1st EDITION

Perspectives on Modern World History

The Atomic Bombings of Hiroshima and Nagasaki

Sylvia Engdahl

Book Editor

GREENHAVEN PRESS
A part of Gale, Cengage Learning

GALE
CENGAGE Learning™

Detroit • New York • San Francisco • New Haven, Conn • Waterville, Maine • London

Christine Nasso, *Publisher*
Elizabeth Des Chenes, *Managing Editor*

© 2011 Greenhaven Press, a part of Gale, Cengage Learning.

Gale and Greenhaven Press are registered trademarks used herein under license.

For more information, contact:
Greenhaven Press
27500 Drake Rd.
Farmington Hills, MI 48331-3535
Or you can visit our Internet site at gale.cengage.com.

For product information and technology assistance, contact us at
Gale Customer Support, 1-800-877-4253.

For permission to use material from this text or product, submit all requests online at
www.cengage.com/permissions.

Further permissions questions can be e-mailed to permissionrequest@cengage.com.

Articles in Greenhaven Press anthologies are often edited for length to meet page requirements. In addition, original titles of these works are changed to clearly present the main thesis and to explicitly indicate the author's opinion. Every effort is made to ensure that Greenhaven Press accurately reflects the original intent of the authors. Every effort has been made to trace the owners of copyrighted material.

Cover image Custom Medical Stock Photo, Inc. Reproduced by permission.

LIBRARY OF CONGRESS CATALOGING-IN-PUBLICATION DATA
The atomic bombings of Hiroshima and Nagasaki / Sylvia Engdahl, book editor.
   p. cm. -- (Perspectives on modern world history)
   Includes bibliographical references and index.
ISBN 978-0-7377-5256-4 (hardcover)
1. Hiroshima-shi (Japan)--History--Bombardment, 1945. 2. Nagasaki-shi (Japan)--History--Bombardment, 1945. 3. Atomic bomb--History--20th century. 4. World War, 1939–1945--Aerial operations, American. I. Engdahl, Sylvia.
  D767.25.H6A88 2011
  940.54'2521954--dc22
                                                      2010051820

Printed in the United States of America
1 2 3 4 5 6 7 15 14 13 12 11

CONTENTS

benefits to mankind, but that only a love of peace can prevent it from being used destructively.

CHAPTER 2

Controversies Surrounding the Atomic Bombings

efforts to persuade the government to demonstrate the atomic bomb rather than use it against Japan, and his belief that if the United States had not used it, the nuclear arms race could have been avoided.

   Max Hastings

   An editorial in a British newspaper on the sixtieth anniversary of the atomic bombing of Hiroshima explains that, although it is now believed that Japan could not have continued the war even if the bomb had not been used, that was not known at the time. It argues that people who find it easy today to condemn the use of the bomb fail to recognize the dilemmas faced by those who made the decision to use it.

   Klaus Wiegrefe

   A German journalist describes the events leading up to the bombings of Hiroshima and Nagasaki for a European audience. He declares that, despite the terrible destruction, the world benefited from the use of the atomic bomb, because it prevented the Cold War from becoming a military war.

   Mark Weber

   A historian argues that Japan was attempting to make peace before the atomic bombs were used, that their use was unnecessary and wrong, and that although most Americans accepted the official justifications, there were critics even at the time.

the atrocities committed by Japan during the war, and that Americans should not take such a dark view of the nation's history.

CHAPTER 3   Personal Narratives

A German priest who was at a Jesuit mission just over a mile from Hiroshima describes the effects of the blast. He describes how he and his fellow priests helped the crowds of wounded who managed to reach their chapel, and how his group made its way into the devastated city to rescue others.

FOREWORD

"History cannot give us a program for the future, but it can give us a fuller understanding of ourselves, and of our common humanity, so that we can better face the future."

—Robert Penn Warren,
American poet and novelist

The history of each nation is punctuated by momentous events that represent turning points for that nation, with an impact felt far beyond its borders. These events—displaying the full range of human capabilities, from violence, greed, and ignorance to heroism, courage, and strength—are nearly always complicated and multifaceted. Any student of history faces the challenge of grasping the many strands that constitute such world-changing events as wars, social movements, and environmental disasters. But understanding these significant historic events can be enhanced by exposure to a variety of perspectives, whether of people involved intimately or of ones observing from a distance of miles or years. Understanding can also be increased by learning about the controversies surrounding such events and exploring hot-button issues from multiple angles. Finally, true understanding of important historic events involves knowledge of the events' human impact—of the ways such events affected people in their everyday lives—all over the world.

Perspectives on Modern World History examines global historic events from the twentieth-century onward by presenting analysis and observation from numerous vantage points. Each volume offers high school, early college level, and general interest readers a thematically arranged anthology of previously published materials that address a major historical event, with an emphasis on international coverage. Each volume opens with background information on the event, then presents the controversies surrounding that event, and concludes with first-person narratives from people who lived through the event or were affected by it. By providing primary sources from the time of the event, as well as relevant commentary surrounding the event, this series can be used to inform debate, help develop critical thinking skills, increase global awareness, and enhance an understanding of international perspectives on history.

Material in each volume is selected from a diverse range of sources, including journals, magazines, newspapers, nonfiction books, personal narratives, speeches, congressional testimony, government documents, pamphlets, organization newsletters, and position papers. Articles taken from these sources are carefully edited and introduced to provide context and background. Each volume of Perspectives on Modern World History includes an array of views on events of global significance. Much of the material comes from international sources and from US sources that provide extensive international coverage.

Each volume in the Perspectives on Modern World History series also includes:

- A full-color **world map**, offering context and geographic perspective.
- An annotated **table of contents** that provides a brief summary of each essay in the volume.
- An **introduction** specific to the volume topic.
- For each viewpoint, a brief **introduction** that has notes about the author and source of the viewpoint, and that provides a summary of its main points.
- Full-color **charts**, **graphs**, **maps**, and other visual representations.

- Informational **sidebars** that explore the lives of key individuals, give background on historical events, or explain scientific or technical concepts.
- A **glossary** that defines key terms, as needed.
- A **chronology** of important dates preceding, during, and immediately following the event.
- A **bibliography** of additional books, periodicals, and Web sites for further research.
- A comprehensive **subject index** that offers access to people, places, and events cited in the text.

Perspectives on Modern World History is designed for a broad spectrum of readers who want to learn more about not only history but also current events, political science, government, international relations, and sociology—students doing research for class assignments or debates, teachers and faculty seeking to supplement course materials, and others wanting to improve their understanding of history. Each volume of Perspectives on Modern World History is designed to illuminate a complicated event, to spark debate, and to show the human perspective behind the world's most significant happenings of recent decades.

INTRODUCTION

The dropping of atomic bombs on the Japanese cities of Hiroshima and Nagasaki in 1945 is one of the most controversial events in US history. Some people believe that this was an act of a different nature than the rest of the military actions during World War II and that it should not have happened. Besides considering it immoral, they believe that the nuclear arms race of later years could have been avoided if atomic bombs had never been used. Others say the exact opposite: In their opinion, the horrific example of the atomic bombings prevented the Cold War from becoming a hot war and that more lives were saved than lost in 1945 because the use of the atomic bombs shortened the war.

Was it worse to kill two hundred thousand people with two bombs than to kill five hundred thousand or more with many bombs? Most people at that time did not think so. To them, as to President Harry S. Truman and his advisors, the secret weapon that had been developed was simply a new bomb, one of awesome power, but no different in the military sense from those already in use. Far more people were killed in the firebombings of Tokyo than died at Hiroshima and Nagasaki combined, and had Japan been invaded, casualties on both sides would have been many times higher. Americans rejoiced that the need for the planned invasion was eliminated.

The concept of nuclear war now familiar to everyone did not exist in 1945. The word "nuke" had not yet been coined. The nuclear weapons developed and stockpiled later were vastly more powerful than the Hiroshima bomb, and their delivery by fleets of planes kept continuously in the air, or by long-range missiles permanently aimed at the cities of nations considered dangerous, was not envisioned by Americans of the 1940s. Today, nuclear war is universally perceived to be a horror to be avoided at all costs, but this is because of hindsight—and foresight—that was unavailable to the people of that era.

The widespread feeling that the atomic bombing of Japan was worse than other bombings arose for several reasons. The first reason was the extent of the suffering and death from radiation poisoning that occurred in the years after the bombing. The American public was not aware initially of the radiation produced by atomic bombs and it was not mentioned in news reports until its results became evident. As time passed and the long-term consequences of radiation exposure were understood, some observers started to think that it might be better to be killed quickly by an ordinary bomb than to die slowly from—or even to live with—the effects of radiation.

Second, people gradually realized what it would mean if not just a few atomic bombs but many were used by both sides in a future war. In 1945, Americans were grateful that Hitler had not gotten the bomb first, a danger the Manhattan Project had been initiated to avert; they realized that would have meant the conquest, and perhaps destruction, of the United States. But they had not yet imagined civilization as a whole being destroyed, much less the entire planet. As nuclear weapons became ever more powerful and were acquired by the Soviet Union as well as the United States, Americans began to feel that perhaps setting a precedent by using the first one had not been a good idea. Whether failure to use it would have made any difference in the future threat is a controversial question.

Third, in the 1960s during the Vietnam War, US war policy in general became a divisive political issue. Critics of it were more numerous—and more outspoken—than had been the case earlier. Many of them looked back and reevaluated the bombing of Hiroshima and Nagasaki, which even the far left had originally supported, and declared that it had been not only unethical but unnecessary.

Was the use of the atomic bombs unnecessary? Opinions are now sharply divided. A lot depends on how one defines "necessary." Certainly it was not necessary to use A-bombs to win the war; it had become obvious that Japan could not win. But it was believed at the time—and many people still believe—that it was necessary to prevent an invasion of Japan that would have involved a catastrophic loss of life on both sides. Although justifications offered for using the atomic bomb generally emphasize the saving of American lives, it saved even more Japanese lives and not just among the armed forces: Civilians, besides living in cities that were being hit with conventional bombs, were being trained to fight off invaders with spears.

In his blog *Sense of Events*, retired Army officer Donald Sensing—now a church pastor—points out that because the US Navy had blockaded Japan, cutting it off from Asian mainland food stocks, the Japanese were close to starvation by late spring 1945. That fall, typhoons damaged Japan's rice fields. If the war had still been going on, the death toll would have been high and the starving people might have rebelled against their government, leading to still more carnage. "Had President Truman not ordered the atom bombings, the US military could have done nothing but intensify conventional bombing and blockading," he writes. "Hence, Japan could not possibly have been brought to a gentler end of the war than the ending that occurred. Had fighting continued after early August 1945, additional civilian deaths would certainly have numbered in the many hundreds of thousands and probably in the millions by the end of the year. More likely, though, is that without the atom bombings, Japan would have become embroiled in civil war, which also would have been lethal beyond estimate."

Some people believe that killing civilians is not justifiable even if it does save the lives of more civilians. Moreover, some historians believe Japan was already about to admit defeat and that the war would not have continued more than a few days even if the A-bombs had not been dropped. No one can be sure about this because the leaders of Japan were not in accord. Some, including Emperor Hirohito, did want to make peace. But, although the Japanese people of that time revered their emperor as a living god, he was not an absolute ruler and could not end the war by decree. It had to be decided by the Japanese Cabinet, which included military leaders who wanted to keep fighting no matter how many of their own people were killed. When the emperor made his desire to surrender clear after the destruction of Hiroshima and Nagasaki, some of the military officers were so adamantly opposed that they tried to overthrow him, an attempt that failed because other officers remained loyal. Would they have, if there had been no atomic bombings? Would the emperor have taken such an unprecedented step as to intervene if he had not been appalled by the suffering caused by what he described as "a most cruel bomb"? Historians disagree about this. As with other crossroads of history, what would have happened if events had followed a different course can never be known for certain.

It has often been observed with respect to the atomic bombings that there is a gulf between the views of people who are old enough to remember World War II and those who were born since. Whatever one thinks about it now, the decision makers of the time should be judged by what was known to them then, not by what is known or believed today.

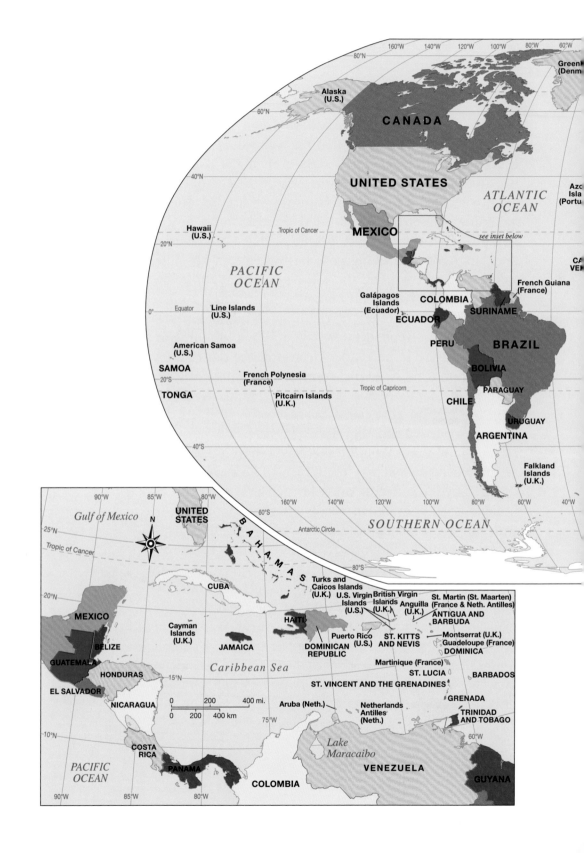

80°N

160°W 140°W 120°W 100°W 80°W 60°W

Green
(Denm

Alaska
(U.S.)

CANADA

60°N

UNITED STATES

ATLANTIC
OCEAN

Azc
Isla
(Portu

40°N

Tropic of Cancer

20°N

Hawaii
(U.S.)

MEXICO

see inset below

CA
VEN

PACIFIC
OCEAN

Galápagos
Islands
(Ecuador)

COLOMBIA

French Guiana
(France)

SURINAME

0°

Equator

Line Islands
(U.S.)

ECUADOR

PERU

BRAZIL

American Samoa
(U.S.)

BOLIVIA

SAMOA

French Polynesia
(France)

20°S

Tropic of Capricorn

PARAGUAY

TONGA

Pitcairn Islands
(U.K.)

CHILE

URUGUAY

ARGENTINA

40°S

Falkland
Islands
(U.K.)

160°W 140°W 120°W 100°W 80°W 60°W 40°W

60°S

Antarctic Circle

SOUTHERN OCEAN

80°S

90°W 85°W 80°W

Gulf of Mexico

UNITED
STATES

N

B
A
H
A
M
A
S

25°N

Tropic of Cancer

CUBA

Turks and
Caicos Islands
(U.K.)

U.S. Virgin
Islands
(U.S.)

British Virgin
Islands
(U.K.)

Anguilla
(U.K.)

St. Martin (St. Maarten)
(France & Neth. Antilles)

ANTIGUA AND
BARBUDA

20°N

MEXICO

Cayman
Islands
(U.K.)

HAITI

JAMAICA

Puerto Rico
(U.S.)

ST. KITTS
AND NEVIS

Montserrat (U.K.)
Guadeloupe (France)
DOMINICA

BELIZE

DOMINICAN
REPUBLIC

GUATEMALA

Caribbean Sea

Martinique (France)

ST. LUCIA

BARBADOS

HONDURAS

15°N

ST. VINCENT AND THE GRENADINES

EL SALVADOR

NICARAGUA

0   200   400 mi.

0   200   400 km

Aruba (Neth.)

GRENADA

Netherlands
Antilles
(Neth.)

TRINIDAD
AND TOBAGO

75°W

10°N

COSTA
RICA

PANAMA

PACIFIC
OCEAN

90°W 85°W 80°W

COLOMBIA

Lake
Maracaibo

VENEZUELA

60°W

GUYANA

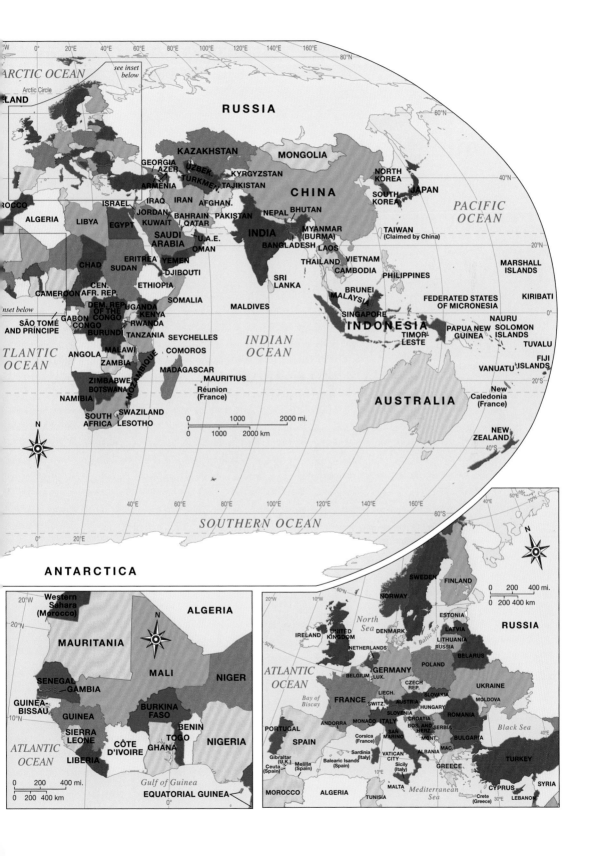

CHAPTER 1

Historical Background on the Atomic Bombings

An Overview of the Atomic Bombings of Hiroshima and Nagasaki

Gale Encyclopedia of World History

The atomic bombings of Hiroshima and Nagasaki on August 6 and 9, 1945, were the only two nuclear attacks in history. They forced the Japanese to surrender, thus ending World War II and saving the thousands of lives that would have been lost in an invasion. The atomic bomb was originally developed because scientists feared that the Nazis would do it first, so they persuaded President Franklin D. Roosevelt to establish the top-secret Manhattan Project. By the time the bomb was ready, Germany had surrendered, and President Harry S. Truman decided to use it against Japan, rejecting a suggestion that it be merely demonstrated. The first bomb killed about seventy thousand people instantly; the second, about forty thousand. Thousands more were injured or left homeless. Emperor Hirohito then prevailed upon the Japanese military leaders to capitulate and broadcast a radio address asking his subjects to "endure the unendurable."

Photo on previous page: The first atomic bomb was dropped on Hiroshima, Japan, by the United States on August 6, 1945. The attack killed 70,000 people instantly and hastened the end of World War II. (**Getty Images.**)

SOURCE. *Gale Encyclopedia of World History: War (2 Volume Set).* © 2008 Gale, a part of Cengage Learning, Inc. Reproduced by permission. www.cengage.com/permissions.

After the German surrender in May [1945], Japan was left with the Allies' undivided attention. The atomic bombings of Hiroshima and Nagasaki, which took place on August 6 and August 9, 1945, forced a Japanese surrender without costing the Allies a bloody invasion of the home islands. The two bombings, which remain the only nuclear attacks in history, ushered in a new age and permanently changed the nature of warfare, politics, and international diplomacy.

The roots of the atomic attacks stretched back to 1939, when a group of scientists, including the famed physicist Albert Einstein (1879–1955), concerned that Germany was developing a program to build atomic weapons, approached President Franklin Roosevelt. Such weapons, the scientists argued, were a theoretical possibility, and the United States would do well to form an exploratory committee with an eye towards developing such technology before the Nazis did.

> The two bombings . . . ushered in a new age and permanently changed the nature of warfare, politics, and international diplomacy.

The Manhattan Project

Roosevelt took their advice, and the exploratory committee developed into the Manhattan Project, a top-secret government effort that funneled $2 billion into building an atomic weapon. Under the guidance of a brain trust of top physicists, the theoretical possibility was on the verge of becoming an atomic reality when President Roosevelt died in April 1945.

Newly sworn-in President Harry Truman was then told of the bomb and its destructive potential. He was further informed that the bomb would be ready in four months. As it turned out, Germany did not last that long, surrendering on May 8. With the intended target of the bomb now out of the war, the question of whether to use the weapon on Japan quickly arose.

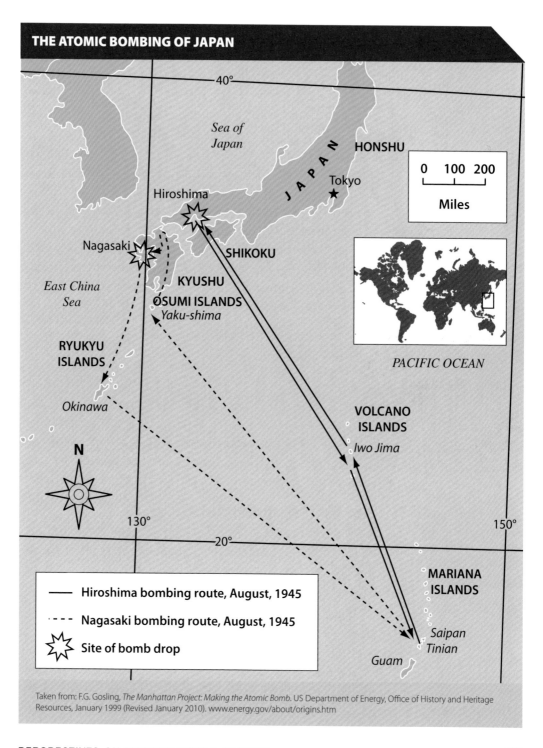

THE ATOMIC BOMBING OF JAPAN

40°

Sea of
Japan

HONSHU

JAPAN

Tokyo

Hiroshima

0   100   200

Miles

Nagasaki

SHIKOKU

East China
Sea

KYUSHU
OSUMI ISLANDS
Yaku-shima

PACIFIC OCEAN

RYUKYU
ISLANDS

Okinawa

VOLCANO
ISLANDS

Iwo Jima

N

130°

150°

20°

MARIANA
ISLANDS

——— Hiroshima bombing route, August, 1945

- - - - Nagasaki bombing route, August, 1945

☆ Site of bomb drop

Saipan
Tinian

Guam

Taken from: F.G. Gosling, *The Manhattan Project: Making the Atomic Bomb.* US Department of Energy, Office of History and Heritage Resources, January 1999 (Revised January 2010). www.energy.gov/about/origins.htm

Hiroshima's Prefectural Industrial Promotion Hall was reduced to a shell by the August 6, 1945 atomic blast that left the city in ruins. (**Associated Press.**)

The Potsdam Declaration

At the victorious Allies' German Potsdam Conference in July 1945, Truman warned Japan to surrender immediately or face "utter devastation," although he did not provide any further details. Meanwhile, in Alamogordo, New Mexico, the first atomic bomb was successfully tested on July 16.

August 1945 was the decisive month of the war in the Pacific. The Soviet Union, in accordance with agreements reached at Yalta, was gearing up to enter the war against Japan. Whether this factored into the American decision to use the atomic bomb is unknown.

What is certain is that the main reason for using the bomb was the goal of a quick surrender of Japan, which would eliminate the need for an invasion of the home islands. Such an invasion was set to begin in November. After the bloodbath on Okinawa, the prospect of fighting two million determined Japanese defending their homeland, backed by 5,000 or more *kamikaze* [suicide] fighters, motivated the Americans to avoid an action that would likely result in millions of deaths and total Japanese casualties in the tens of millions.

> The main reason for using the bomb was the goal of a quick surrender of Japan, which would eliminate the need for an invasion of the home islands.

Several options for demonstrating the bomb's capabilities in a non-lethal way—detonating it in front of a panel of international observers or dropping it into Tokyo Bay—were dismissed because a detonation failure would only strengthen Japanese resolve.

Truman authorized the use of the bomb in early August. A target committee had selected several cities that were both military and psychological targets, and from this list the city of Hiroshima, an important military-industrial center, emerged as the primary target, in part because it was the only city on the list without a POW camp.

Hiroshima and Nagasaki

In the early morning hours of August 6, 1945, the B-29 *Enola Gay* took off from its base on Tinian with an escort of two other bombers carrying instrumentation and photography equipment. By 08:15 A.M., the bombers were over Hiroshima and the bomb was released. The blast, equivalent to 12,500 tons of TNT, created a fireball that reached 5,400 degrees Fahrenheit and killed around 70,000 people instantly. Outside the one-mile blast radius, fires quickly began to spread, eventually burning down four square miles of the city.

On August 8, as authorities in Tokyo began to slowly appreciate what had just happened, the Soviet Union entered the war, invading Manchuria and scything through the Japanese Kwangtung Army stationed there. The following day, ahead of a predicted weeklong period of bad weather, a second bomb was hurriedly dropped on the city of Nagasaki. The second blast was somewhat contained by the hills around the epicenter; at least 40,000 people were killed outright, including some survivors of the Hiroshima blast who had fled that city three days before.

Japanese Surrender

The Japanese government, which had been making conditional peace overtures through Moscow, agreed to a near-unconditional surrender at the behest of Emperor Hirohito. The only condition the Japanese now insisted on was the preservation of the Imperial line. This was agreed to and Hirohito made a radio address on August 14—after a militarist coup attempted to stop the broadcast—announcing Japan's capitulation and asking his disbelieving subjects to "endure the unendurable."

The relative roles that the atomic bombs and the Soviet invasion played in the Japanese decision to surrender have been a source of endless debate. Even Japanese officials, in postwar interviews, seemed to give conflicting assessments. Regardless of the effectiveness of the atomic attacks, the suffering they unleashed cannot be denied.

In the confused hours after the attack on Hiroshima, Radio Tokyo supplied some of the first accounts of the aftermath of the bombing:

> With the gradual restoration of order following the disastrous ruin that struck the city of Hiroshima in the wake of the enemy's new-type bomb on Monday morning, the authorities are still unable to obtain a definite checkup on the extent of the casualties sustained by the

civilian population. Medical relief agencies that were rushed from neighboring districts were unable to distinguish, much less identify, the dead from the injured. The impact of the bomb was so terrific that practically all living things, human and animal, were literally seared to death by the tremendous heat and pressure engendered by the blast. All the dead and injured were burned beyond recognition. With houses and buildings crushed, including the emergency medical facilities, the authorities are having their hands full in giving every available relief under the circumstances. The effect of the bomb was widespread. Those outdoors burned to death while those indoors were killed by the indescribable pressure and heat.

The First Test Explosion of an Atomic Bomb

US War Department

On July 16, 1945, an atomic bomb was tested for the first time. The following press release was issued by the US War Department later, after the existence of the bomb had been announced. It describes in detail the test and what led up to it, emphasizing how much more spectacular it was than most observers had expected. The scientists emotionally congratulated each other because a job that had seemed impossible had finally been accomplished, resolving that this powerful new force should always be used for good. They agreed that, whatever else might happen, it would now be possible to end the war quickly and save thousands of American lives.

Mankind's successful transition to a new age, the Atomic Age, was ushered in July 16, 1945, before the eyes of a tense group of renowned scientists and military men gathered in the desertlands

SOURCE. "War Department Press Release on New Mexico Test, July 16, 1945," US War Department, 1945.

of New Mexico to witness the first end results of their $2,000,000,000 effort. Here in a remote section of the Alamogordo Air Base 120 miles southeast of Albuquerque, the first man-made atomic explosion, the outstanding achievement of nuclear science, was achieved at 5:30 A.M. of that day. Darkening heavens, pouring forth rain and lightning immediately up to the zero hour, heightened the drama.

Mounted on a steel tower, a revolutionary weapon destined to change war as we know it, or which may even be the instrumentality to end all wars, was set off with an impact which signalized man's entrance into a new physical world. Success was greater than the most ambitious estimates. A small amount of matter, the product of a chain of huge specially constructed industrial plants, was made to release the energy of the universe locked up within the atom from the beginning of time. A fabulous achievement had been reached. Speculative theory, barely established in pre-war laboratories, had been projected into practicality.

This phase of the Atomic Bomb Project, which is headed by Major General Leslie R. Groves, was under the direction of Dr. J.R. Oppenheimer, theoretical physicist of the University of California. He is to be credited with achieving the implementation of atomic energy for military purposes.

Tension before the actual detonation was at a tremendous pitch. Failure was an ever-present possibility. Too great a success, envisioned by some of those present, might have meant an uncontrollable, unusable weapon.

Assembling the Bomb

Final assembly of the atomic bomb began on the night of July 12 in an old ranch house. As various component assemblies arrived from distant points, tension among the scientists rose to an increasing pitch. Coolest of all was the man charged with the actual assembly of the

vital core, Dr. R.F. Bacher, in normal times a professor at Cornell University.

The entire cost of the project, representing the erection of whole cities and radically new plants spread over many miles of countryside, plus unprecedented experimentation, was represented in the pilot bomb and its parts. Here was the focal point of the venture. No other country in the world had been capable of such an outlay in brains and technical effort.

The full significance of these closing moments before the final factual test was not lost on these men of science. They fully knew their position as pioneers into another age. They also knew that one false move would blast them and their entire effort into eternity. Before the assembly started, a receipt for the vital matter was signed by Brigadier General Thomas F. Farrell, General Groves' deputy. This signalized the formal transfer of the irreplaceable material from the scientists to the Army.

During final preliminary assembly, a bad few minutes developed when the assembly of an important section of the bomb was delayed. The entire unit was machine-tooled to the finest measurement. The insertion was partially completed when it apparently wedged tightly and would go no farther. Dr. Bacher, however, was undismayed and reassured the group that time would solve the problem. In three minutes' time, Dr. Bacher's statement was verified and basic assembly was completed without further incident.

Specialty teams, comprised of the top men on specific phases of science, all of which were bound up in the whole, took over their specialized parts of the assembly. In each group was centralized months and even years of channelized endeavor.

On Saturday, July 14, the unit which was to determine the success or failure of the entire project was elevated to the top of the steel tower. All that day and the next, the job of preparation went on. In addition to the apparatus

Photo on previous page: The people who pioneered the atomic bomb—including Leon Smith, shown here with a replica of the weapon used on Nagasaki—did so under intense secrecy. (Associated Press.)

necessary to cause the detonation, complete instrumentation to determine the pulse beat and all reactions of the bomb was rigged on the tower.

A Tense Countdown

The ominous weather which had dogged the assembly of the bomb had a very sobering effect on the assembled experts whose work was accomplished amid lightning flashes and peals of thunder. The weather, unusual and upsetting, blocked out aerial observation of the test. It even held up the actual explosion scheduled at 4:00 A.M. for an hour and a half. For many months the approximate date and time had been set and had been one of the high-level secrets of the best kept secret of the entire war.

> All present were ordered to lie on the ground, face downward, heads away from the blast direction.

[The] nearest observation point was set up 10,000 yards south of the tower, where in a timber and earth shelter the controls for the test were located. At a point 17,000 yards from the tower at a point which would give the best observation, the key figures in the atomic bomb project took their posts. . . .

At three o'clock in the morning the party moved forward to the control station. General Groves and Dr. Oppenheimer consulted with the weathermen. The decision was made to go ahead with the test despite the lack of assurance of favorable weather. The time was set for 5:30 A.M.

General Groves rejoined Dr. [James B.] Conant and Dr. [Vannevar] Bush, and just before the test time they joined the many scientists gathered at the Base Camp. Here all present were ordered to lie on the ground, face downward, heads away from the blast direction.

Tension reached a tremendous pitch in the control room as the deadline approached. The several observation points in the area were tied in to the control room by radio. . . .

The time signals, "minus 20 minutes, minus fifteen minutes," and on and on increased the tension to the breaking point as the group in the control room which included Dr. Oppenheimer and General Farrell held their breaths, all praying with the intensity of the moment which will live forever with each man who was there. At "minus 45 seconds," robot mechanism took over and from that point on the whole great complicated mass of intricate mechanism was in operation without human control. Stationed at a reserve switch, however, was a soldier scientist ready to attempt to stop the explosion should the order be issued. The order never came.

A Blinding Flash

At the appointed time there was a blinding flash lighting up the whole area brighter than the brightest daylight. A mountain range three miles from the observation point stood out in bold relief. Then came a tremendous sustained roar and a heavy pressure wave which knocked down two men outside the control center. Immediately thereafter, a huge multi-colored surging cloud boiled to an altitude of over 40,000 feet. Clouds in its path disappeared. Soon the shifting substratosphere winds dispersed the now grey mass.

The test was over, the project a success.

The steel tower had been entirely vaporized. Where the tower had stood, there was a huge sloping crater. Dazed but relieved at the success of their tests, the scientists promptly marshalled their forces to estimate the strength of America's new weapon. To examine the nature of the crater, specially equipped tanks were wheeled into the area, one of which carried Dr. Enrico Fermi, noted nuclear scientist. Answer to their findings rests in the destruction effected in Japan today in the first military use of the atomic bomb.

'The feeling of the entire assembly, even the uninitiated, was of profound awe.'

Had it not been for the desolated area where the test was held and for the cooperation of the press in the area, it is certain that the test itself would have attracted far-reaching attention. As it was, many people in that area are still discussing the effect of the smash. A significant aspect, recorded by the press, was the experience of a blind girl near Albuquerque many miles from the scene, who, when the flash of the test lighted the sky before the explosion could be heard, exclaimed, "What was that?" . . .

Profound Awe

[General Groves said,] "The feeling of the entire assembly, even the uninitiated, was of profound awe. Drs. Conant and Bush and myself were struck by an even stronger feeling that the faith of those who had been responsible for the initiation and the carrying on of this Herculean project had been justified."

General Farrell's impressions are: "The scene inside the shelter was dramatic beyond words. . . . For some hectic two hours preceding the blast, General Groves stayed with the Director. Twenty minutes before the zero hour, General Groves left for his station at the base camp, first because it provided a better observation point and second, because of our rule that he and I must not be together in situations where there is an element of danger which existed at both points.

"Just after General Groves left, announcements began to be broadcast of the interval remaining before the blast to the other groups participating in and observing the test. As the time interval grew smaller and changed from minutes to seconds, the tension increased by leaps and bounds. Everyone in that room knew the awful potentialities of the thing that they thought was about to happen. The scientists felt that their figuring must be right and that the bomb had to go off but there was in everyone's mind a strong measure of doubt.

"We were reaching into the unknown and we did not know what might come of it. It can safely be said that most of those present were praying—and praying harder than they had ever prayed before. If the shot were successful, it was a justification of the several years of intensive effort of tens of thousands of people—statesmen, scientists, engineers, manufacturers, soldiers, and many others in every walk of life.

"In that brief instant in the remote New Mexico desert, the tremendous effort of the brains and brawn of all these people came suddenly and startlingly to the fullest fruition. Dr. Oppenheimer, on whom had rested a very heavy burden, grew tenser as the last seconds ticked off. He scarcely breathed. He held on to a post to steady himself. For the last few seconds, he stared directly ahead and then when the announcer shouted 'Now!' and there came this tremendous burst of light followed shortly thereafter by the deep growling roar of the explosion, his face relaxed into an expression of tremendous relief. Several of the observers standing back of the shelter to watch the lighting effects were knocked flat by the blast.

> 'There was a feeling in that shelter that those concerned with [atomic fission's] nativity should dedicate their lives to the mission that it would always be used for good and never for evil.'

The Birth of a New Age

"The tension in the room let up and all started congratulating each other. Everyone sensed 'This is it!' No matter what might happen now all knew that the impossible scientific job had been done. Atomic fission would no longer be hidden in the cloisters of the theoretical physicists' dreams. It was almost full grown at birth. It was a great new force to be used for good or for evil. There was a feeling in that shelter that those concerned with its nativity should dedicate their lives to the mission that it would always be used for good and never for evil.

"Dr. [George] Kistiakowsky [another key member of the project] threw his arms around Dr. Oppenheimer and embraced him with shouts of glee. Others were equally enthusiastic. All the pent-up emotions were released in those few minutes and all seemed to sense immediately that the explosion had far exceeded the most optimistic expectations and wildest hopes of the scientists. All seemed to feel that they had been present at the birth of a new age— The Age of Atomic Energy—and felt their profound responsibility to help in guiding into right channels the tremendous forces which had been unlocked for the first time in history.

"As to the present war, there was a feeling that no matter what else might happen, we now had the means to insure its speedy conclusion and save thousands of American lives. As to the future, there had been brought into being something big and something new that would prove to be immeasurably more important than the discovery of electricity or any of the other great discoveries which have so affected our existence.

"The effects could well be called unprecedented, magnificent, beautiful, stupendous and terrifying. No man-made phenomenon of such tremendous power had ever occurred before. The lighting effects beggared description. The whole country was lighted by a searing light with the intensity many times that of the midday sun. It was golden, purple, violet, gray and blue. It lighted every peak, crevasse and ridge of the nearby mountain range with a clarity and beauty that cannot be described but must be seen to be imagined. It was that beauty the

> 'A searing light with the intensity many times that of the midday sun . . . lighted every peak, crevasse and ridge of the nearby mountain range with a clarity and beauty that cannot be described but must be seen to be imagined.'

great poets dream about but describe most poorly and inadequately. Thirty seconds after, the explosion came first, the air blast pressing hard against the people and things, to be followed almost immediately by the strong, sustained, awesome roar which warned of doomsday and made us feel that we puny things were blasphemous to dare tamper with the forces heretofore reserved to the Almighty. Words are inadequate tools for the job of acquainting those not present with the physical, mental and psychological effects. It had to be witnessed to be realized."

The US President Announces the Atomic Bombing of Hiroshima

Harry S. Truman

Americans first heard about the atomic bombing of Hiroshima from a White House press release prepared by President Harry S. Truman while he was sailing home from the Potsdam Conference, a meeting of Allied leaders in occupied Germany. This statement, broadcast over the radio and summarized in newspapers across the nation, was the first public announcement of the existence of such a bomb. In it, Truman explains the nature of the secret project that led to the release of atomic energy and praises the work of the many people who took part, calling it the greatest scientific achievement in history. He concludes by recommending that Congress establish a commission to control the use of atomic power for the maintenance of world peace.

SOURCE. "Harry S. Truman, White House Press Release," Trumanlibrary.org, courtesy of Harry S. Truman Library.

Sixteen hours ago an American airplane dropped one bomb on Hiroshima, an important Japanese Army base. That bomb had more power than 20,000 tons of T.N.T. It had more than two thousand times the blast power of the British "Grand Slam" which is the largest bomb ever yet used in the history of warfare.

The Japanese began the war from the air at Pearl Harbor. They have been repaid many fold. And the end is not yet. With this bomb we have now added a new and revolutionary increase in destruction to supplement the growing power of our armed forces. In their present form these bombs are now in production and even more powerful forms are in development.

> The force from which the sun draws its power has been loosed against those who brought war to the Far East.

It is an atomic bomb. It is a harnessing of the basic power of the universe. The force from which the sun draws its power has been loosed against those who brought war to the Far East.

A Scientific Gamble

Before 1939, it was the accepted belief of scientists that it was theoretically possible to release atomic energy. But no one knew any practical method of doing it. By 1942, however, we knew that the Germans were working feverishly to find a way to add atomic energy to the other engines of war with which they hoped to enslave the world. But they failed. We may be grateful to Providence that the Germans got the V-1s and V-2s [missiles] late and in limited quantities and even more grateful that they did not get the atomic bomb at all.

The battle of the laboratories held fateful risks for us as well as the battles of the air, land and sea, and we have now won the battle of the laboratories as we have won the other battles.

President Truman's Radio Speech on the Atomic Bombing of Japan

After returning from the Potsdam Conference, President Harry S. Truman delivered an often-quoted radio speech to the nation. It included the following comments about the atomic bomb.

The British, Chinese, and United States Governments have given the Japanese people adequate warning of what is in store for them. We have laid down the general terms on which they can surrender. Our warning went unheeded; our terms were rejected. Since then the Japanese have seen what our atomic bomb can do. They can foresee what it will do in the future.

The world will note that the first atomic bomb was dropped on Hiroshima, a military base. That was because we wished in this first attack to avoid, insofar as possible, the killing of civilians. But that attack is only a warning of things to come. If Japan does not surrender, bombs will have to be dropped on her war industries and, unfortunately, thousands of civilian lives will be lost. I urge Japanese civilians to leave industrial cities immediately, and save themselves from destruction.

I realize the tragic significance of the atomic bomb.

Its production and its use were not lightly undertaken by this Government. But we knew that our enemies were on the search for it. We know now how close they were to finding it. And we

Beginning in 1940, before Pearl Harbor, scientific knowledge useful in war was pooled between the United States and Great Britain, and many priceless helps to our victories have come from that arrangement. Under that general policy the research on the atomic bomb was begun. With American and British scientists working together we entered the race of discovery against the Germans.

The United States had available the large number of scientists of distinction in the many needed areas of knowledge. It had the tremendous industrial and financial resources necessary for the project and they could knew the disaster which would come to this Nation, and to all peace-loving nations, to all civilization, if they had found it first. . . .

Having found the bomb we have used it. We have used it against those who attacked us without warning at Pearl Harbor, against those who have starved and beaten and executed American prisoners of war, against those who have abandoned all pretense of obeying international laws of warfare. We have used it in order to shorten the agony of war, in order to save the lives of thousands and thousands of young Americans.

We shall continue to use it until we completely destroy Japan's power to make war. Only a Japanese surrender will stop us. . . .

We must constitute ourselves trustees of this new force—to prevent its misuse, and to turn it into the channels of service to mankind.

It is an awful responsibility which has come to us. We thank God that it has come to us, instead of to our enemies; and we pray that He may guide us to use it in His ways and for His purposes.

SOURCE. *Harry S. Truman Library and Museum, Public Papers, "Radio Report to the American People on the Potsdam Conference," August 9, 1945. www.trumanlibrary.org/publicpapers/index.php?pid=104&st=&st1=*

be devoted to it without undue impairment of other vital war work. In the United States the laboratory work and the production plants, on which a substantial start had already been made, would be out of reach of enemy bombing, while at that time Britain was exposed to constant air attack and was still threatened with the possibility of invasion. For these reasons Prime Minister [Winston] Churchill and President [Franklin] Roosevelt agreed that it was wise to carry on the project here. We now have two great plants and many lesser works devoted to the production of atomic power. Employment during peak construction numbered 125,000 and over 65,000 individuals

> We have spent two billion dollars on the greatest scientific gamble in history—and won.

are even now engaged in operating the plants. Many have worked there for two and a half years. Few know what they have been producing. They see great quantities of material going in and they see nothing coming out of these plants, for the physical size of the explosive charge is exceedingly small. We have spent two billion dollars on the greatest scientific gamble in history—and won.

A Historic Achievement

But the greatest marvel is not the size of the enterprise, its secrecy, nor its cost, but the achievement of scientific brains in putting together infinitely complex pieces of knowledge held by many men in different fields of science into a workable plan. And hardly less marvelous has been the capacity of industry to design, and of labor to operate, the machines and methods to do things never done before so that the brain child of many minds came forth in physical shape and performed as it was supposed to do. Both science and industry worked under the direction of the United States Army, which achieved a unique success in managing so diverse a problem in the advancement of knowledge in an amazingly short time. It is doubtful if such another combination could be got together in the world. What has been done is the greatest achievement of organized science in history. It was done under high pressure and without failure.

We are now prepared to obliterate more rapidly and completely every productive enterprise the Japanese have above ground in any city. We shall destroy their docks, their factories, and their communications. Let there be no mistake; we shall completely destroy Japan's power to make war.

It was to spare the Japanese people from utter destruction that the ultimatum of July 26 [1945] was issued

at Potsdam. Their leaders promptly rejected that ultimatum. If they do not now accept our terms they may expect a rain of ruin from the air, the like of which has never been seen on this earth. Behind this air attack will follow sea and land forces in such numbers and power as they have not yet seen and with the fighting skill of which they are already well aware.

The Secretary of War, who has kept in personal touch with all phases of the project, will immediately make public a statement giving further details.

President Harry S. Truman announces the Japanese surrender on August 14, 1945, less than a week after the atomic bombings of Hiroshima and Nagasaki. (Associated Press.)

His statement will give facts concerning the sites at Oak Ridge near Knoxville, Tennessee, and at Richland near Pasco, Washington, and an installation near Santa Fe, New Mexico. Although the workers at the sites have been making materials to be used in producing the greatest destructive force in history they have not themselves been in danger beyond that of many other occupations, for the utmost care has been taken of their safety.

A New Era Has Begun

The fact that we can release atomic energy ushers in a new era in man's understanding of nature's forces. Atomic energy may in the future supplement the power that now comes from coal, oil, and falling water, but at present it cannot be produced on a basis to compete with them commercially. Before that comes there must be a long period of intensive research.

It has never been the habit of the scientists of this country or the policy of this Government to withhold from the world scientific knowledge. Normally, therefore, everything about the work with atomic energy would be made public.

But under present circumstances it is not intended to divulge the technical processes of production or all the military applications, pending further examination of possible methods of protecting us and the rest of the world from the danger of sudden destruction.

I shall recommend that the Congress of the United States consider promptly the establishment of an appropriate commission to control the production and use of atomic power within the United States. I shall give further consideration and make further recommendations to the Congress as to how atomic power can become a powerful and forceful influence towards the maintenance of world peace.

The Atomic Bombing of Hiroshima Is Described in the Press

Chicago Tribune

The following news story published two days after the atomic bombing of Hiroshima provides the first description of it that Americans would read. It was based on a press conference with Paul Tibbets, the pilot, and weapons officer William Parsons, who designed the firing mechanism for the bomb and armed it in flight. They told reporters about the work that led up to the flight, as well as what was seen from the air. Generals Carl Spaatz and Curtis LeMay, who also appeared at the press conference, were obviously encouraged by the success of the new weapon. They guardedly discussed its effectiveness but refused to conjecture specifically on how the bomb would affect the end of the war with Japan.

SOURCE. "Atom Bomb Crew's Story," *Chicago Tribune*, 1945. Reproduced by permission.

Crewmen of the Super Fort from which the first atomic bomb in the history of war was dropped on the Japanese city of Hiroshima Aug. 6 [1945] said today the new weapon struck with a flash and concussion that brought an exclamation of "My God" from the battle-hardened airmen 10 miles away.

There are more B-29s ready to carry more of the same awesome bombs from their bases in the Marianas [islands in the Pacific Ocean] in a follow-up on other enemy targets. This was announced by Gen. Spaatz, commander of the United States army strategic air force. Spaatz said there would be a leaflet campaign to let the Japanese people know they had been atom-bombed and could expect more.

> Crewmen who carried the new bomb . . . although they were far away, felt the concussion like a close explosion of anti-aircraft fire.

Like Close Explosion

Crewmen who carried the new bomb, which is declared to have an explosive power the equivalent of bombs that 2,000 Super Fortresses would have had to carry previously, although they were far away, felt the concussion like a close explosion of anti-aircraft fire.

Col. Paul W. Tibbets Jr. of Quincy, Ill., and Miami, Fla., who piloted the Super Fortress, and Chicago born Navy Capt. William S. Parsons, now of Santa, Fe, N.M., navy ordnance expert, described the explosions as "tremendous and awe inspiring."

"It was 0915 (9:15 A.M.) when we dropped our bomb and we turned the plane broadside to get the best view," said Capt. Parsons, who has the title of "weaponeer." "Then we made as much distance from the ball of fire as we could.

"We were at least 10 miles away and there was a visual impact, even though every man wore colored glasses for protection. We had braced ourselves when the bomb was gone for the shock and Tibbets said 'close flak' and it was just like that—a close burst of anti-aircraft fire.

"The crew said, 'My God,' and couldn't believe what had happened.

Mountain of Smoke Rises

"A mountain of smoke was going up in a mushroom with the stem coming down. At the top was white smoke but up to 1,000 feet from the ground there was swirling, boiling dust. Soon afterward small fires sprang up on the edge of town but the town was entirely obscured. We stayed around two or three minutes and by that time the smoke had risen to 40,000 feet.

"As we watched the top of the white cloud broke off and another soon formed."

The tall, balding navy officer told of his reaction to his first atomic bomb flight with the calmness of a professor lecturing to a group of students on butterflies. He is the man who actually designed the [firing mechanism for the] bomb.

Beginning in June, 1943, he worked to perfect an explosive of such tremendous force that could be carried with comparative safety in a plane for as long as it takes to fly from the Marianas to Japan. Parsons said it was good psychology from the outset to have the person in charge of designing the bomb know that he was to go along on the first battle mission.

Bomb Not Controllable

A little more than a year elapsed between the first tryout in New Mexico and the first atomic bombing. Parsons said so many facsimiles had been dropped experimentally that when the great moment over the target came yesterday he could hardly realize it was the real thing.

The "weaponeer" explained that the atomic bomb is not controllable like the ordinary bomb, but he could not, of course, go into detail.

SANTA FE NEW MEXICAN

The Oldest Newspaper in the Southwest, Founded in 1849

SANTA FE, NEW MEXICO, MONDAY, AUGUST 6, 1945

Price 5c

Los Alamos Secret Disclosed by Truman

ATOMIC BOMBS DROP ON JAPAN

Deadliest Weapons in World's History Made In Santa Fe Vicinity

By WILL HARRISON

Santa Fe learned officially today of a city of 6,000 in its own front yard.

The reverberating announcement of the Los Alamos bomb, with 2,000 times the power of the great Grand-Slammers dropped on Germany, also lifted the secret of the community on the Pajarito Plateau, whose presence Santa Fe has ignored, except in whispers, for more than two years.

'Utter Destruction,' Promised in Potsdam Ultimatum, Unleashed; Power Equals 2,000 Superforts

WASHINGTON, Aug. 6 (AP)—The U. S. Army Air Force has released on the Japanese an atomic bomb containing more power than 20,000 tons of TNT.

It produces more than 2,000 times the blast of the largest bomb ever used before.

The announcement of the development was made in a statement by President Truman released by the White House today.

The bomb was dropped 16 hours ago on Hiroshima, an important Japanese army base.

The President said that the bomb has "added a new and revolutionary increase in destruction" on the Japanese.

Mr. Truman added:

"It is an atomic bomb. It is a harnessing of the basic power of the universe. The force from which the sun draws its power has been loosed against those who brought war to the Far East."

May Be Tool To End Wars; New Era Seen

4 More Nippon Cities Now Smoldering Ruins

American airmen and 'big force' four more forewarned Japanese cities to ashes today as 790 Superforts and Mustang fighters reportedly swept the enemy's sacred islands with this bomb, rockets and parachute bombs.

Hi Johnson Dies at 79

WASHINGTON, Aug. 6 (AP)—Hiram W. Johnson of California, militant opponent of the League of Nations and the San Francisco Charter for a United Nations organization, died today.

Tomato Juice Off Rationing

WASHINGTON, Aug. 6 (AP)—Canned and bottled tomato juice today goes off rationing.

Now They Can Be Told Aloud, Those Stoories of 'the Hill'

By WILLIAM McNULTY

The secret of Los Alamos is out and The New Mexican staff and other newspapermen through New Mexico can have a sigh—sigh—nothing, it's more of a gloat—of relief.

The Weather

As close as Parsons has been associated with the top secret project, he was in the dark about some phases of it. After reading background material distributed among the correspondents, he commented, "I learned a lot from this handout."

Details of the bombing were disclosed at a press conference attended by Gen. Spaatz, who termed the new bomb the "most revolutionary development in the history of the world."

Spaatz was obviously highly elated at the new bombing weapon. He said if he had had it in Europe, "It would have shortened the war six to eight months." Maj. Gen. Curtis LeMay said that if this bomb had been available there would have been "no need to have had D-day in Europe."

LeMay, former commanding general of the 20th air force, is chief of staff under Spaatz.

Known Only to Three Men

The Super Fortress which carried the bomb took off from a Marianas base and only three men knew what they carried—Col. Tibbets, Capt. Parsons, and the bombardier, Maj. Thomas W. Ferebee, [of] Mocksville, N.C. Other crewmen knew only that it was a highly secret, important mission.

Tibbets had been trained specially for this mission, which Gen. Spaatz considered so vital he awarded Tibbets the distinguished service cross as he stepped from his plane after the flight. The plane was named "Enola Gay," after Tibbets' mother in Miami.

There were many secrets about the flight and the bombing which followed. One secret was the selection of Hiroshima as the target. It was believed probable, however, that it was selected not because of its great importance but partly because the weather was clear there and visibility was such as to permit a close watch of the bomb explosion.

Photo on previous page: The dropping of the Hiroshima bomb lifted a great curtain of secrecy from the weapon's development and use. (**Corbis**.)

No difficulty was encountered in reaching the target.

Best of Facilities

"When we went out we had the best of facilities made available to us," Tibbets said.

"The bomb run up to the target was uneventful and there were no disturbing elements in the bomb run when the release was made.

> Officers discussed guardedly the possible effectiveness of the new bomb which was described as giving off intense heat for some distance around it.

"We saw a flash, felt the concussions and it reminded me of a close burst of flak. We stayed in the target area looking at the scene below and the towering column of smoke. I have never seen anything like it."

Other members of the crew were Capt. Robert A. Lewis, Ridgefield Park, N.J., airplane commander; Capt. Theodore J. Van Kirk, Northumbreland, Pa., navigator; 2d. Lt. Morris Jeppson, electronics officer; Sgt. Joe A. Stiborik, Taylor, Tex., radar operator; Sgt. Robert R. Shumard, Detroit, Mich., gunner and assistant flight engineer; Staff Sgt. Wyatt E. Dusenberry, Lansing, Mich., flight engineer; Pvt. Richard H. Nelson, Los Angeles, Cal., radio operator; and Staff Sgt. George R. Caron, central fire control gunner.

Discussion of the size or other features of the atomic bomb wasn't permitted, but it is carried by a single Super Fortress.

Spaatz, LeMay, and other general officers discussed guardedly the possible effectiveness of the new bomb which was described as giving off intense heat for some distance around it. In experiments in New Mexico, the heat was said to have been felt 20 miles away.

One officer described it as essentially an air weapon when asked if it would be possible to be used by the

Arming the Atomic Bomb During Flight

Navy Captain William "Deak" Parsons, leader of the Ordnance Division for the Manhattan Project, is less famous than the eminent scientists who developed the atomic bomb and the pilot of the plane that dropped it, but it was he who designed the mechanism for setting it off and personally armed the bomb in flight. The following is a portion of the official letter, dated September 19, 1945, awarding him the Army Silver Star.

After takeoff in the very early morning hours, the plane set course as planned. Captain Parsons then climbed into the bomb bay to set the powder charge, which had been postponed until well after takeoff to assure the safety of the island from which departure had been made. The job was completed without incident in forty minutes. As the aircraft approached Japan the risks grew greater, for the element of hazard from the unknown was ever present, since this was the first time this bomb, much more destructive than any in existence, had been released from an airplane. The possibilities of damage from anti-aircraft fire, enemy fighters, and unforeseen failures added to the risk; nor was it certain what effect detonation would have upon the bomber and its occupants. Accompanying the mission to insure the bomb's correct use, Captain Parsons kept watch until the plane was in its briefed position, and then approved release. At 0915 the switch was pressed, the bomb cleared safely, and fell towards its planned objective. They then departed with speed from the target area, traveling a safe distance before the blast occurred. By his high degree of skill in directing work with the atomic bomb, and great personal risk in placing the powder charge in the bomb during flight, Captain Parsons distinguished himself, reflecting the highest credit on himself and the United States Navy.

SOURCE. *Facsimile of letter at www.arlingtoncemetery.net/wparsons.htm.*

fleet. Parsons was asked whether a bomb was capable of starting tidal waves. He said if it were dropped in the sea, there would be a lot of waves and high geysers but expressed doubt that it would start a tidal wave.

Another officer said that "Its effect probably would be disappointingly slight on shipping."

Granting the tremendous power of the atomic bomb, Spaatz refused to conjecture specifically on how it would affect the end of the war with Japan, but said: "It won't be pleasant for the Japanese to absorb."

Atomic Energy Must Be Used Responsibly

George Fielding Eliot

In the following viewpoint, George Fielding Eliot reports on the atomic bombing of Hiroshima two days after it occurred. He says it may prove to be the most important scientific discovery of all time and may alter the history of the human race. He had no information at the time on the exact degree of destruction caused by the bomb and speculates that the purpose of the bombing may have been to give the Japanese a foretaste of what might happen as additional atomic bombs are produced. He considers it a sign of God's providence that the weapon is in the hands of the Allies and not Germany or Japan. The immense responsibility that lies on the United States cannot be overemphasized, he says. Eliot was a major in the US Army and the author of many books on military and political issues, as well as a syndicated column. He was the military analyst for CBS News during World War II.

SOURCE. George Fielding Eliot, "Atomic Bomb May Alter History of the Human Race," *Los Angeles Times*, 1945. Reproduced by permission.

The harnessing of atomic energy to the uses of man may well prove the most important scientific discovery of all time.

For good or ill it well may alter the history of the human race. But for the moment the industrial and hence the social changes which may be brought about by this primal power lie well in the future. With its military uses we are immediately concerned, because it is to military ends that its discovery is first of all being turned.

The military uses of atomic power may be considered under two heads: Its immediate application to the Japanese war and its effect on the maintenance of peace by the United Nations organization.

Effects Evaluated

Its effect on the Japanese war seems likely to be in proportion to the degree to which it can be brought to bear on Japanese targets. In the first use of a new weapon, a decision always has to be made as to the time of its employment against the enemy.

The contention on this point is always between those who want to begin experiment as soon as the thing is at all usable and those who want to wait until a sufficient stock is in hand to gain a great advantage if it works as advertised, thus reaping to the full the effect of surprise.

On the one hand, it is always urged that laboratory experiment is never as good a test as actual use in the field so that the earlier field experiment begins, the more rapid the subsequent application of the new weapon will be. On the other hand, it is always contended that the first use gives the enemy information of what is in store for him and he begins at once to work out countermeasures.

Validity Doubted

Whether this latter contention has much validity in the present case is to be doubted, for it would seem a matter

Photo on following page: In 1945 constructive uses of nuclear power were unrealized, but the energy source took on global importance later in the twentieth century. (David Wasserman/Getty Images.)

of great difficulty, if not impossibility, for the Japanese in their present straits to work out any worthwhile defenses against the terrible weapon with which they are now being assailed. Hence it is quite possible that we have made a small beginning which is indeed further suggested by the fact that the first important test in the United States took place on July 16 [1945], and the first atomic bomb was dropped on Japan only about three weeks thereafter. The purpose may therefore be to give the Japanese an immediate foretaste of what is coming to them later on as additional supplies of the atomic bombs become available.

Destruction Gauge

Word as to the exact degree of destruction effected at Hiroshima may thus be of the very first importance and may have an appreciable hearing on the further duration of the Japanese war.

It looks as if the atomic bomb attack on Hiroshima is a part of a scheduled operation directed against the will to fight of the Japanese people—first the three-power ultimatum, then the Japanese refusal, then the scheduled bombing of Japanese cities "by roster," then the Potsdam communique outlining the fate which the German people brought upon themselves by obeying their war lords to the bitter end, now the announcement of the atomic bomb and its first use against Hiroshima.

After War's End, What?

While we wait for the news of what happened to Hiroshima—if that city of 300,000 souls any longer exists—it may well be considered what is going to happen when the Japanese war is ended. We may assume that the atomic bomb will hasten the end of the war, at least, if it does not terminate it abruptly. What then?

The free peoples of the world now have in their possession a weapon so terrible that for the present, at least, nothing can stand against it. The saving grace in this situation, the outward and visible sign of God's merciful providence, is that this weapon is in the hands of the American, British, and Canadian peoples, and not in the hands of a Hitler or a Japanese war lord.

Truman's Words Quoted

In this connection, the closing words of President [Harry] Truman's statement are of immense significance: "Under present circumstances it is not intended to divulge the technical processes of production of all the military applications, pending further examination of possible methods of protecting us and the rest of the world from the danger of sudden destruction. I shall recommend that the Congress consider promptly the establishment of an appropriate commission to control the production and use of atomic power within the United States. I shall give further consideration and make further recommendations to the Congress as to how atomic power can become a powerful and forceful influence toward the maintenance of world peace."

> No scientific discovery, no mere instrument will save us from ourselves . . . if we are as a nation too stupid, too hesitant, or too indifferent to make use of what we have for the benefit of mankind.

Immense Responsibility

The immense responsibility which now lies on the shoulders of those peoples whose representatives must make the decisions suggested by the President can hardly be overemphasized. We must realize what this responsibility means. No scientific discovery, no mere instrument will save us from ourselves if we are false to our duty; if we are as a nation too stupid, too hesitant, or too indifferent to make use of what we have for the benefit of mankind. In the last analysis, the basic factor is still the human factor.

Must Sacrifice for Freedom

Free we are, and free we are determined to remain. But we cannot remain so just by saying so. We have seen the sacrifices which our freedom has demanded of us in two great wars because we had not the wit and the energy to take the steps which might have prevented them. We have had our lesson; we have paid a bitter price for it, and now we have a new and awe-inspiring opportunity to establish and to defend it. But to do that, we must rise superior in our hearts and our souls to the frightful forces our minds have unleashed on this shrinking planet— forces which may be turned to our use or to our destruction. The choice is ours.

> We must rise superior in our hearts and our souls to the frightful forces our minds have unleashed on this shrinking planet.

The British Reaction to the Atomic Bombing of Hiroshima

Sunday Times *(London)*

In a farsighted article published two days after the atomic bombing of Hiroshima, Britain's major newspaper, the *Times*, declares that it will be a long time before the full significance of "this vast and mysterious power" is known. It argues that atomic power could put an end to civilization unless mankind adopts a positive love of peace. But that, if the world succeeds in controlling it, atomic power could bring more material enrichment of life than any previous scientific discovery, abolishing servile toil and bestowing undreamed-of riches to all people.

An impenetrable cloud of dust and smoke, standing over the ruin of the great Japanese arsenal at Hiroshima, still veils the undoubtedly stupen-

---

SOURCE. "Darkness Over Hiroshima," *Sunday Times* (London), August 8, 1945. http://archive.timesonline.co.uk. Reproduced by permission.

The power from atomic fission can wreak immense destruction—or serve the needs of industry and civilization. (**Associated Press.**)

dous destruction wrought by the first impact in war of the atomic bomb. A mist no less impenetrable is likely for a long time to conceal the full significance in human affairs of the release of the vast and mysterious power hitherto locked within the infinitesimal units of which the material structure of the universe is built up. All that can be said with certainty is that the world stands in the presence of a revolution in earthly affairs at least as big with potentialities of good and evil as when the forces of steam or electricity were harnessed for the first time to the purposes of industry and war.

The Urgency of War Hastens Scientific Discovery

It has to be sorrowfully acknowledged that these epoch-making conquests of science are no sooner achieved than they are turned to the purposes of mutual destruction. Thus war battens on peace. This time, however, it is the pressure of war itself that has forced ahead a process which can be turned against war in the long run and at the same time promises a greater material enrichment of life than any single scientific discovery before it. Science itself is neutral, like the blind forces of nature that it studies and aspires to control. Nations fighting for their existence, however, seek to make science their ally by enlisting men of science in their service. As men of science they seek only truth, but as patriots in the hour of their country's danger they are legitimately called upon to deflect their researches as policy and strategy require. The immense expenditure incurred in the quest of the atomic bomb—that is to say the immense share of the total manpower and material resources of the allied nations put at the disposal of the comparatively few scientists directing the quest—amounting as it has done to two thousand million dollars, is out of all proportion to anything that scientific research can command in time of peace. There is no need to interpret this fact cynically; these vast sums were risked—for the project was, as President Truman says, "a gamble"—as a means to ensure the survival of a civilization in which the disinterested pursuit of knowledge might again be made secure. But . . . the urgencies of war have but hastened—probably by many years—a discovery that the great physicists of the world have long foreseen, and towards which they have been moving by the patient processes of the laboratory for many years past.

Imagination shudders at the thought that this terrifying power might have fallen into the hands of the enemies of civilization instead of its protectors. It is known that Nazi Germany was seeking frantically after the secret; and many gallant British and Norwegian lives were spent in thwarting the design. The allies, however, have a right to feel that it is no accident which won them the momentous race. They have achieved an outstanding intellectual victory over the enemy, and it is a victory that comes to them by right. It is significant that two of the outstanding scientists named as collaborators in the Anglo-American programme of experiment were German subjects exiled from their country on the ground of race. Pre-eminence in the pursuit of knowledge must belong to a social system in which men, whatever their origin, are free to follow "whithersoever the argument may lead"; in the intellectual sphere, as on the battlefield, the discipline of free minds has its inalienable advantage.

> Beyond all doubt, unless atomic power is turned to serve the aims of peace, it can speedily make an end of civilized life on earth.

Atomic Power Must Be Used to End War and Serve Peace

Speculation can only peer a little way into the future that the new power opens for the world. The issue of the Japanese war, already certain, must be greatly hastened, whether the rulers of Tokyo acknowledge by surrender the demonstration that the allies hold them in the hollow of their hand, or insist on immolating their country before the irresistible power of the new weapon, which is amply acknowledged in their latest broadcasts. If they choose the second alternative, it seems likely that the allies may be able to accomplish, what [Gerd von] Rundstedt [general field marshal of the German army during World War II] is said to have expected to achieve against Britain, the destruction of Japanese resistance in the home islands by air power alone, leaving to the army the role of occupation only. Beyond the Japanese war the consequences for strategy and grand tactics are vast but incalculable. Presumably all fortification, as it has been hitherto understood, becomes immediately obsolete; for nothing can resist the new force. Schemes for world security founded on the maintenance of bases at the strategic points of the globe will call for exhaustive reconsideration.

All strategic calculation, however, becomes insignificant before the evident challenge to the people of the world to rise to the fateful occasion in such degree as to make strategy itself speedily irrelevant. Beyond all doubt, unless atomic power is turned to serve the aims of peace, it can speedily make an end of civilized life on earth. It will not serve those aims through the mere dissemination of the knowledge that renewal of war now means universal destruction and collapse. History, especially the history of recent times in which the instruments of destruction and torment have so rapidly multiplied, holds out no expectation that men will ever be deterred from war by fear alone; and on the whole that is to the credit of human nature. If the secular curse is to be laid, it must be by the positive love of peace. Reason will tell mankind that war is becoming with certainty suicidal. But reason will no more avail than the appeal to fear. Humanity must be able to call upon deeper convictions. All that can be directly expected because of the existence of the new terrifying power is a livelier sense among statesmen and the peoples to whom they are answerable of the weight of the responsibility of choosing between peace and war.

> It is not yet known . . . whether we must look forward to a time when a few individual enemies of society can equip themselves to wield these devastating powers.

This is to say that so terrible a power must be brought and kept under responsible control. It cannot be a segregated or specialized control, distinct from the control of war itself. It is not yet known whether the new weapon will always require for its production the great resources of a national state, or whether we must look forward to a time when a few individual enemies of society can equip themselves to wield these devastating powers. But in either case there is no salvation in the attempt to confine the scientific knowledge now achieved to a few trusted people. That way lies only underground competition in diabolical devices, ending with a fresh cataclysm. Moreover, as the President of the Royal Society [the chief scientific organization of Britain] argues in his letter this morning, it would be treason to the spirit of science itself. Humanity must bear the burden of its own power. There is no alternative but that the world authority already in process of constitution [i.e., the United Nations, which was being formed at the time], with the mission of fostering a self-discipline in the human race that may abolish recourse to the arbitrament of war, must continue its task with the added understanding of the appalling forces it has to hold in check. To fail is finally "to shut the gates of mercy on mankind."

> [Atomic power] holds without doubt the potentiality of reducing the physical labour needed to sustain life to a small fraction of what is now required.

Great Potential for the Peaceful Use of Atomic Power

To succeed, on the other hand, is to open to future generations unimaginable vistas of material progress. The fundamental power of the universe, the power manifested in the sunshine that has been recognized from the remotest ages as the sustaining force of earthly life, is entrusted at last to human hands. Many, perhaps very many, years of further research may be required before the atomic force, so devastating in its untamed state, can be domesticated to the peaceful uses of man. But it holds without doubt the potentiality of reducing the physical labour needed to sustain life to a small fraction of what is now required, of bestowing undreamed of riches upon all men, of abolishing servile or mechanical toil, and of creating universal leisure for the cultivation of the higher ends of the mind and spirit. All these things are attainable—but are not offered as a free gift. The condition of their enjoyment, that the new power be consecrated to peace and not to war, is a choice set before the conscience of humanity; and in a terrible and most literal sense it is a choice of life or death.

CHAPTER 2

Controversies Surrounding the Atomic Bombings

The Atomic Bombings Were Justified Because They Saved Many Lives

Andrew Kenny

In the following viewpoint, South African journalist Andrew Kenny describes his feelings during his visit to Hiroshima in 2005, saying that in his opinion US President Harry S. Truman was right to drop the atomic bomb on Japan because it saved millions of lives—American, British, and Japanese. The Japanese would not have surrendered without it, as they were prepared to accept 100 million deaths during an invasion. After the war, the United States forced democracy on Japan and this has worked well, he says, as the Japanese are now peaceful, healthy, and prosperous. Kenny contends that chronic radiation effects from the bomb were quite small and there has been no genetic damage at all. Although the atomic bombing was terrible, more people were killed in World War II in conventional bombing and in Rwanda's 1994 conflict with weapons as simple as machetes and clubs. Kenny, formerly a senior research officer at the

Photo on previous page: The remains of Hiroshima following the atomic bombings. The Prefectural Industrial Promotion Hall is now known as the A-Bomb Dome and is the centerpiece of a war memorial. (Getty Images.)

SOURCE. Andrew Kenny, "Why This Was a Good Day for Mankind," *Daily Mail* (London), 2005. Reproduced by permission.

Energy Research Institute of the University of Cape Town in South Africa, is now an independent energy consultant.

A *dragonfly flitted in front of me and stopped on a fence. I stood up, took my cap in my hands, and was about to catch the insect when . . .*

. . . there was a flash of white light in the blue sky above Hiroshima. This was at 8:15 A.M. on August 6, 1945.

Then followed a new kind of thunder and a new kind of hellfire. A minute later, those who were still alive, those whose flesh was not falling off their bodies, blinked into a changed world, like a traveller waking and finding himself on a different planet.

Through the glare of flames and the darkness of smoke, they saw that their city had vanished, to be replaced by a blackened desert, empty of everything except fire, charcoal, corpses and the concrete skeletons of buildings.

Some of the dead had become small: shrivelled lumps of charred meat sticking to pavements and bridges. Some of the living had become big: swollen red monsters with pits in their faces where their eyes and mouths had been.

A man without feet walked on his ankles; a woman without a jaw stood with her tongue hanging out of her head; a naked man sat holding his eyeball in his hand. One of the crew of the bomber, describing what he had seen below, said: "Did you ever go to the beach and stir up the sand in shallow water and see it all billow up? That's what it looked like to me." Sixty-six thousand people died instantly, 120,000 by the end of the year.

A Visit to Hiroshima

I visited Hiroshima last month. I was in Kyoto to attend an energy conference where, somewhat ironically, I suppose, I gave a talk on South Africa's new nuclear

power plant, the Pebble Bed Modular Reactor (it was well received).

After the conference, I took the train to Hiroshima, swishing through the Japanese countryside at 180 mph in a spotlessly clean and comfortable carriage.

A conductor in a demure uniform bowed to us upon entering and leaving it. I looked out at the low hills of Japan with their feathery covering of light green trees, and at the neat grey towns with factories and paddy fields in their midst.

At Hiroshima station I took the tram to the most haunting ruin in the world and then walked through a graceful park to the "Peace Museum" (the war museum).

Conventional bombs dropped on Germany and Japan—including ones that ignited the Tokyo firestorm depicted above by painter Teruo Kanoh—killed more people than atomic bombs did. (Associated Press.)

The museum is sombre, informative and horrifying. Models and large photographs show the city before and after the bomb.

There are statistics of death, heat, pressure and radiation, eyewitness accounts of children watching their mothers die in front of them, anecdotes—such as the man about to catch the dragonfly—and little household relics such as molten spoons and a wristwatch stopped at 8:15 A.M.

But the most evocative remnant stands outside the museum on a riverbank. It is the ruin of the Hiroshima Prefectural Industrial Promotion Hall, usually known as the "Atomic Dome."

Hiroshima is built on a large delta consisting of seven rivers. At its centre is the T-shaped Aioi Bridge, which provides a three-way crossing where one river divides into two.

This T was the target for the atomic bombardier. As intended, the bomb exploded 600 yards above the ground, but it was slightly out in direction by 200 yards to the south.

The Promotion Hall is close to the bridge. It was built in 1915, designed by a Czech architect, and consisted of cylindrical shapes joined together into a four-storey block with a small green dome on the top. It looked like half an apple on top of a jukebox. The atomic bomb vastly improved it as an aesthetic object, changing it from a mundanely ugly building into a masterpiece of stricken form.

I gazed at it for a long time from every angle and then paced out the distance south to where the bomb had gone off. In an act of compulsive foolishness, I stared upward to look for the spot in the air.

The Bomb Saved Millions of Lives

Was U.S. President Harry Truman right to drop it? I have no doubt he was.

However I look at it, I cannot see other than that the bomb saved millions of lives, Allied and Japanese.

All British combatants in World War II that I have ever spoken to, including my parents, described the same reaction when they heard of the Hiroshima bomb: tremendous relief.

Tommy, a foreman of a factory I worked at in Lancashire in 1980, told me that in July 1945 he was in the Pacific doing exercises for the invasion of Japan. He expected to die. He thanked the bomb that he became a grandfather.

> "The invasion of Japan itself would probably have been the bloodiest episode in human combat. . . . Japanese Imperial Headquarters called for '100 million deaths with honour.'"

The most effective soldiers in the war were the Germans. The only way the Allies could beat them was to outnumber and outgun them. They seemed to have a limitless supply of officers with quick, flexible minds who could read a battle and make a swift and intelligent assessment of the best tactics required.

For the opposite reason, the Japanese were among the most ineffective soldiers in the war. Tough, brave and stoical, they became useless as battle winners if you killed their commander.

They could not think for themselves and, without orders and leaders, became a ferocious and implacable mob, hopeless for securing victory but terrifyingly dangerous in refusing defeat.

They would not surrender. The casualties when the Americans invaded the outlying islands in the Pacific held by the Japanese were sickeningly high because they just refused to surrender.

The invasion of Japan itself would probably have been the bloodiest episode in human combat. Expecting it, Japanese Imperial Headquarters called for "100 million deaths with honour."

Japanese Civilian Leaders Used the Atomic Bombing to End the War

According to some Japanese historians, Japanese civilian leaders who favored surrender saw their salvation in the atomic bombing. The Japanese military was steadfastly refusing to give up, so the peace faction seized on the bombing as a new argument to force surrender. Koichi Kido, one of Emperor Hirohito's closest advisors, stated that, "We of the peace party were assisted by the atomic bomb in our endeavor to end the war." Hisatsune Sakomizu, the chief Cabinet secretary in 1945, called the bombing "a golden opportunity given by heaven for Japan to end the war." According to these historians and others, the pro-peace civilian leadership was able to use the destruction of Hiroshima and Nagasaki to convince the military that no amount of courage, skill and fearless combat could help Japan against the power of atomic weapons.

SOURCE. *"Atomic Bombings of Hiroshima and Nagasaki," WordIQ Encyclopedia, 2010. www.wordiq.com/definition/ Atomic_bombings_of_Hiroshima_and_Nagasaki.*

Making things worse was the chaotic leadership of Japan. The country's "15-Year War" had not been started by political leaders, but by two mad colonels in Manchuria.

We shall never know what happened at command level in Japan during the war because documents were destroyed before the Allied occupation, but there certainly was murderous conflict between generals, admirals and politicians.

The Emperor was the only one with supreme authority, even if he lacked will, and we are lucky he survived. Killing Hitler would have shortened the war; killing Emperor Hirohito would have lengthened it.

He was for making peace but needed a special reason for doing so, something so overwhelming that he could face down the generals who wanted to continue the war. The threat of the Soviet Union's joining the war against Japan was not enough. The atomic bomb was.

> " [Emperor Hirohito] was for making peace but needed . . . something so overwhelming that he could face down the generals who wanted to continue the war. "

The first bomb was dropped on Hiroshima on August 6 [1945]. The second was dropped on Nagasaki on August 9. Were they necessary? I'm afraid so.

There was still dithering and defiance after the first bomb, and the American idea was to keep on blowing until the enemy's flame went out. The Americans hurried to roll out the Nagasaki bomb, wanting to give an impression of continued, massive and irresistible destruction.

The third bomb would be ready to fall by August 17. But on August 15, the Emperor announced the surrender.

Democracy in Modern Japan

The U.S. forced democracy on Japan. It worked like a charm and, with enduring peace, achieved a happy wonder.

The Japanese, always industrious and inventive, became model democrats—tolerant, peaceful and considerate. The grandsons of men who abused British prisoners in PoW camps now treat their grandsons with respect and decency.

There is an obvious improvement in health in Japan.

One glance at a Japanese crowd shows a striking difference between generations: those over 60 [years of age] are very short; those under 40 are of Western heights, with six-footers not standing out at all.

Japan has reached new levels of manufacturing prowess and efficiency, improving the whole world with its marvellous products.

The casualties of Hiroshima were mainly from blast and heat. Radiation killed far fewer and these mostly suffered acute damage from the massive direct radiation that struck fast-growing cells in the gut, skin, marrow, blood and in foetuses, causing hideous deaths and abnormalities.

> In the history of human sorrow, the atomic bombs on Japan must be ranked large, but by no means largest. More people were killed in the conventional bombing of Germany and Tokyo.

Chronic radiation effects, the long-lasting effects, were quite small. By 1990, the total number of survivors from both bombs who died from cancer caused by the radiation was estimated at 428—an average of ten a year since the bombs were dropped.

The figure for genetic damage done by the radiation is more precisely known. It is zero. No increase in genetic defects in children born to survivors who conceived after the bomb has ever been seen. . . .

The Atomic Bombs Killed Fewer People than Other Events

In the history of human sorrow, the atomic bombs on Japan must be ranked large, but by no means largest.

More people were killed in the conventional bombing of Germany and Tokyo.

More than twice as many were killed with machetes and clubs in Rwanda in 1994. Mao Tse-tung killed a hundred times more simply by denying people food.

A medieval torturer could match any individual horror of Hiroshima, and personally I should prefer to face an atomic bomb than a man with a redhot poker and a pair of pincers.

The only different thing about the bomb is that so much destruction can be caused so quickly from one source. This is why it ended World War II.

We do not know what happened to that dragonfly 60 years ago. Without the bomb, she might have ended that day as a corpse, stuck to a board with a pin through her chest.

Perhaps, like Tommy the foreman, the bomb saved her life, and her descendants now flit into the future just above the gentle plains of Hiroshima.

The Atomic Bombings Ended the Savagery of Both Sides

Paul Fussell

In the following viewpoint, Paul Fussell argues that those who object to the use of the atomic bomb against Japan are usually people with no combat experience and many who have never been in the armed forces at all. In his opinion, critics have no appreciation of what an invasion would have cost in lives nor of the extent of the brutality practiced by both sides while the war continued. Soldiers were thankful for the atomic bomb, he says, and did not feel guilt or shame as is sometimes assumed. Although the destruction of Hiroshima and Nagasaki was a terrible tragedy, Fussell feels that US President Harry S. Truman should not be blamed in retrospect for making a decision based on strong reasons. Fussell is a professor emeritus of English literature at the University of Pennsylvania. He is the author of many books on cultural and literary history.

Photo on following page: Both sides in the Pacific conflict killed prisoners of war; the Japanese were known to behead them (shown bound is captured Australian pilot Leonard Siffleet, 1916–1943). (**Time & Life Pictures**/**Getty Images.**)

SOURCE. Paul Fussell, "Thank God for the Atom Bomb," *Thank God for the Atom Bomb and Other Essays*. Summit Books, 1988. Reproduced by permission.

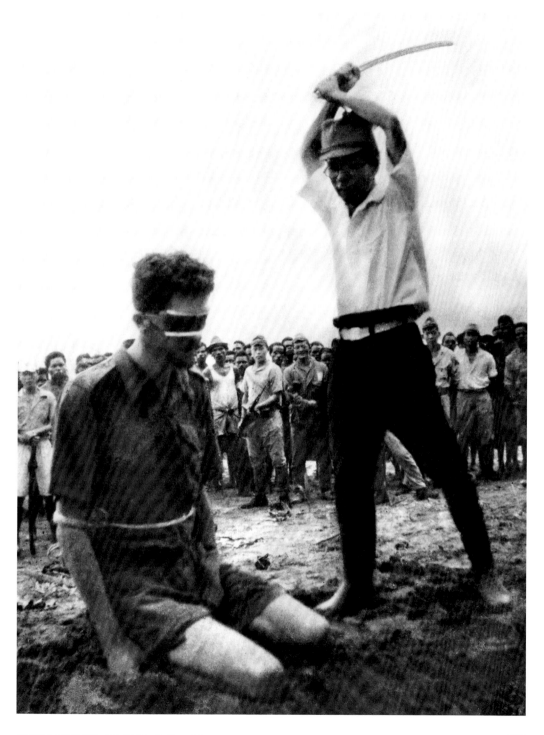

Writing on the forty-second anniversary of the atom-bombing of Hiroshima and Nagasaki, I want to consider something suggested by the long debate about the ethics, if any, of that ghastly affair. Namely, the importance of experience, sheer, vulgar experience, in influencing, if not determining, one's views about that use of the atom bomb.

The experience I'm talking about is having to come to grips, face to face, with an enemy who designs your death. The experience is common to those in the marines and the infantry and even the line navy, to those, in short, who fought the Second World War mindful always that their mission was, as they were repeatedly assured, "to close with the enemy and destroy him." *Destroy*, notice: not hurt, frighten, drive away, or capture. I think there's something to be learned about that war, as well as about the tendency of historical memory unwittingly to resolve ambiguity and generally clean up the premises, by considering the way testimonies emanating from real war experience tend to complicate attitudes about the most cruel ending of that most cruel war. . . .

[Journalist] Arthur T. Hadley said recently that those for whom the use of the A-bomb was "wrong" seem to be implying "that it would have been better to allow thousands on thousands of American and Japanese infantrymen to die in honest hand-to-hand combat on the beaches than to drop those two bombs." People holding such views, he notes, "do not come from the ranks of society that produce infantrymen or pilots." And there's an eloquence problem: most of those with firsthand experience of the war at its worst were not elaborately educated people. Relatively inarticulate, most have remained silent about what they know. That is, few of those destined to be blown to pieces if the main Japanese islands had been invaded went on to become our most effective men of letters or impressive ethical theorists or professors of contemporary history or of international law. . . .

An Invasion of Japan Would Have Been Bloody

Former Pfc. E.B. Sledge, author of the splendid memoir *With the Old Breed at Peleliu and Okinawa,* noticed at the time that the fighting grew "more vicious the closer we got to Japan," with the carnage of Iwo Jima and Okinawa worse than what had gone before. He points out that

> what we had *experienced* [my emphasis] in fighting the Japs (pardon the expression) on Peleliu and Okinawa caused us to formulate some very definite opinions that the invasion . . . would be a ghastly bloodletting. . . . It would shock the American public and the world. [Every Japanese] soldier, civilian, woman, and child would fight to the death with whatever weapons they had, rifle, grenade, or bamboo spear.

The Japanese pro-invasion patriotic song, "One Hundred Million Souls for the Emperor," says Sledge, "meant just that." Universal national kamikaze was the point. One kamikaze pilot, discouraged by his unit's failure to impede the Americans very much despite the bizarre casualties it caused, wrote before diving his plane onto an American ship, "I see the war situation becoming more desperate. All Japanese must become soldiers and die for the Emperor." Sledge's First Marine Division was to land close to the Yokosuka Naval Base, "one of the most heavily defended sectors of the island." The marines were told, he recalls, that

> due to the strong beach defenses, caves, tunnels, and numerous Jap suicide torpedo boats and manned mines, few Marines in the first five assault waves would get ashore alive—my company was scheduled to be in the first and second waves. The veterans in the outfit felt we had already run out of luck anyway. . . . We viewed the invasion with complete resignation that we would be killed—either on the beach or inland.

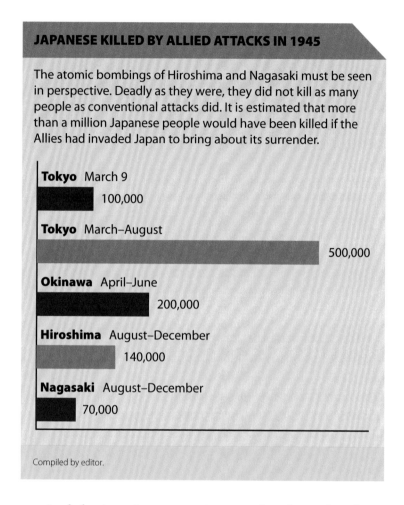

JAPANESE KILLED BY ALLIED ATTACKS IN 1945

The atomic bombings of Hiroshima and Nagasaki must be seen in perspective. Deadly as they were, they did not kill as many people as conventional attacks did. It is estimated that more than a million Japanese people would have been killed if the Allies had invaded Japan to bring about its surrender.

Tokyo March 9
100,000

Tokyo March–August
500,000

Okinawa April–June
200,000

Hiroshima August–December
140,000

Nagasaki August–December
70,000

Compiled by editor.

And the invasion was going to take place: there's no question about that. It was not theoretical or merely rumored in order to scare the Japanese. By July 10, 1945, the prelanding naval and aerial bombardment of the coast had begun, and the battleships *Iowa, Missouri, Wisconsin*, and *King George V* were steaming up and down the coast, softening it up with their sixteen-inch shells.

On the other hand, [economist] John Kenneth Galbraith is persuaded that the Japanese would have surrendered surely by November without an invasion. He thinks the A-bombs were unnecessary and unjustified because the war was ending any way. The A-bombs meant, he says, "a difference, at most, of two or three weeks." But at the time, with no indication that surrender was on the way, the kamikazes were sinking American vessels, the *Indianapolis* was sunk (880 men killed), and Allied casualties were running to over 7,000 per week. "Two or three weeks," says Galbraith. Two weeks more means 14,000 more killed and wounded, three weeks more, 21,000. Those weeks mean the world if you're one of those thousands or related to one of them. During the time between the dropping of the Nagasaki bomb on August 9 and the actual surrender on the fifteenth, the war pursued its accustomed course: on the twelfth of August eight captured American fliers were executed (heads chopped off); the fifty-first United States submarine, *Bonefish*, was sunk (all aboard drowned); the destroyer *Callaghan* went down, the seventieth to be sunk; and the Destroyer Escort *Underhill* was lost. That's a bit of what happened in six days of the two or three weeks posited by Galbraith. What did he do in the war? He worked in the Office of Price Administration in Washington. I don't demand that he experience having his ass shot off. I merely note that he didn't.

Lack of Combat Experience Affects Opinion

Likewise, the historian Michael Sherry, author of a recent book on the rise of the American bombing mystique, *The Creation of Armageddon*, argues that we didn't delay long enough between the test explosion in New Mexico and the mortal explosions in Japan. More delay would have made possible deeper moral considerations and perhaps laudable second thoughts and restraint. "The risks of delaying the bomb's use," he says, "would have been small— not the thousands of casualties expected of invasion but only a few days or weeks of relatively routine operations." While the mass murders represented by these "relatively routine operations" were enacting, Michael Sherry was safe at home. Indeed, when the bombs were dropped he was going on eight months old, in danger only of falling out of his pram [baby carriage]. In speaking thus of Galbraith and Sherry, I'm aware of the offensive implications *ad hominem* [criticizing a person's character instead of his opinions]. But what's at stake in an infantry assault is so entirely unthinkable to those without the experience of one, or several, or many, even if they possess very wide-ranging imaginations and warm sympathies, that experience is crucial in this case.

> The farther from the scene of horror, the easier the talk.

In general, the principle is, the farther from the scene of horror, the easier the talk. One young combat naval officer close to the action wrote home in the fall of 1943, just before the marines underwent the agony of Tarawa: "When I read that we will fight the Japs for years if necessary and will sacrifice hundreds of thousands if we must, I always like to check from where he's talking: it's seldom out here." That was [future US president] Lieutenant (j.g.) John F. Kennedy. And [British prime minister] Winston Churchill, with an irony perhaps too broad and easy, noted in Parliament that the people who preferred invasion to A-bombing seemed to have "no intention of proceeding to the Japanese front themselves." . . .

And not just a staggering number of Americans would have been killed in the invasion. Thousands of British assault troops would have been destroyed too. . . . "But for the atomic bombs," a British observer intimate with the Japanese defenses notes, "I don't think we would have stood a cat in hell's chance. We would have been murdered in the biggest massacre of the war. They would have annihilated the lot of us."

The Dutchman Laurens van der Post had been a prisoner of the Japanese for three and a half years. He and thousands of his fellows, enfeebled by beriberi and pellagra [vitamin deficiencies], were being systematically starved to death, the Japanese rationalizing this treatment not just because the prisoners were white men but because they had allowed themselves to be captured at all and were therefore moral garbage. In the summer of 1945 Field Marshal [Hisaichi] Terauchi issued a significant order: at the moment the Allies invaded the main islands, all prisoners were to be killed by the prison-camp commanders. But thank God that did not happen. When the A-bombs were dropped, van der Post recalls, "This cataclysm I was certain would make the Japanese feel that they could withdraw from the war without dishonor, because it would strike them, as it had us in the silence of our prison night, as something supernatural."

In an exchange of views not long ago in *The New York Review of Books*, [journalist] Joseph Alsop and [historian] David Joravsky set forth the by now familiar argument on both sides of the debate about the "ethics" of the bomb. It's not hard to guess which side each chose once you know that Alsop experienced capture by the Japanese at Hong Kong early in 1942, while Joravsky came into no deadly contact with the Japanese. . . .

Alsop focuses on the power and fanaticism of War Minister [Korechika] Anami, who insisted that Japan fight to the bitter end, defending the main islands with the same techniques and tenacity employed at Iwo [Jima] and Okinawa. Alsop concludes: "Japanese surrender could never have been obtained, at any rate without the honor-satisfying bloodbath envisioned by . . . Anami, if the hideous destruction of Hiroshima and Nagasaki had not finally galvanized the peace advocates into tearing up the entire Japanese book of rules." The Japanese plan to deploy the undefeated bulk of their ground forces, over two million men, plus 10,000 kamikaze planes, plus the elderly and all the women and children with sharpened spears they could muster in a suicidal defense makes it absurd, says Alsop, to "hold the common view, by now hardly challenged by anyone, that the decision to drop the two bombs on Japan was wicked in itself, and that President [Harry] Truman and all others who joined in making or who [like [Mahattan Project physicist] Robert Oppenheimer] assented to this decision shared in the wickedness." And in explanation of "the two bombs," Alsop adds: "The true, climactic, and successful effort of the Japanese peace advocates . . . did not begin in deadly earnest until *after* the second bomb had destroyed Nagasaki. The Nagasaki bomb was thus the trigger to all the developments that led to peace." . . .

David Joravsky, now a professor of history at Northwestern, argued on the other hand that who decided to use the A-bombs on cities betray defects of "reason and self-restraint." It all needn't have happened, he says, "if the U.S. government had been willing to take a few more days and to be a bit more thoughtful in opening up the age of nuclear warfare." . . .

There Was Brutality on Both Sides

The dramatic postwar Japanese success at hustling and merchandising and tourism has (happily, in many ways) effaced for most people the vicious assault context in which the Hiroshima horror should be viewed. It is easy to forget, or not to know, what Japan was like before it was first destroyed, and then humiliated, tamed, and constitutionalized by the West. "Implacable, treacherous, barbaric"—those were Admiral [William] Halsey's characterizations of the enemy, and at the time few facing the Japanese would deny that they fit to a T. One remembers the captured American airmen—the lucky ones who escaped decapitation—locked for years in packing crates. One remembers the gleeful use of bayonets on civilians, on nurses and the wounded, in Hong Kong and Singapore. Anyone who actually fought in the Pacific recalls the Japanese routinely firing on medics, killing the wounded (torturing them first, if possible), and cutting

The Japanese Attitude Toward Death During War

It seems strange to Americans that Japan's military leaders intended to fight on after it was obvious that they could not win the war and that a US invasion of Japan would lead to large numbers of their own people being killed. But death in war was not viewed the same in the Japanese culture as in the West. Under the samurai tradition it was considered to be the only honorable option in the face of defeat; warriors who surrendered were not thought worthy of respect. When Japan did surrender, a number of senior officials, including General Korechika Anami, the War Minister, committed ritual suicide.

Suicide was not at all unusual among the Japanese of that era. In fact, there were far more volunteers for kamikaze missions—the deliberate crashing of bomb-laden planes into enemy ships—than there were planes available; young pilots vied for the honor and received a ceremonial send-off from cheering onlookers. During the Battle of Saipan, when civilians who died there were promised equal spiritual status in the afterlife with those of soldiers perishing in combat, 10,000 of them killed themselves, some by jumping from cliffs. On the island of Okinawa, mass suicides were not merely encouraged but forced—an incident now being deleted from Japanese textbooks under protest from present-day Okinawans. "In many places, parents, children, relatives and friends were ordered or coerced to kill each other in large groups," reads the caption of a display at the Okinawa Prefectural Peace Memorial Museum. "These killings were in the wake of years of militaristic education, which exhorted people to serve their nation by giving their lives to the emperor."

Plans for repelling an invasion of Japan called for 10,000 more kamikaze attacks from the air plus the use of manned torpedoes. Civilians were being taught to become suicide bombers and throw themselves under advancing tanks; women, children, and the elderly were armed with grenades or bamboo spears and told to die fighting. Psychologist Satoshi Kanazawa, writing in *Psychology Today*'s blog on August 21, 2008, says the dropping of the atomic bombs saved the lives of 100 million Japanese and calls it "an act of utmost compassion."

> The degree to which Americans register shock and extraordinary shame about the Hiroshima bomb correlates closely with lack of information about the Pacific war.

off the penises of the dead to stick in the corpses' mouths. The degree to which Americans register shock and extraordinary shame about the Hiroshima bomb correlates closely with lack of information about the Pacific war.

And of course the brutality was not just on one side. There was much sadism and cruelty, undeniably racist, on ours. (It's worth noting in passing how few hopes blacks could entertain of desegregation and decent treatment when the U.S. Army itself slandered the enemy as "the little brown Jap.") Marines and soldiers could augment their view of their own invincibility by possessing a well-washed Japanese skull, and very soon after Guadalcanal it was common to treat surrendering Japanese as handy rifle targets. . . . In the Pacific the situation grew so public and scandalous that in September 1942, the Commander in Chief of the Pacific Fleet issued this order: "No part of the enemy's body may be used as a souvenir. Unit Commanders will take stern disciplinary action. . . ."

Among Americans it was widely held that the Japanese were really subhuman, little yellow beasts, and popular imagery depicted them as lice, rats, bats, vipers, dogs, and monkeys. What was required, said the Marine Corps journal *The Leatherneck* in May 1945, was "a gigantic task of extermination." The Japanese constituted a "pestilence," and the only appropriate treatment was "annihilation." Some of the marines landing on Iwo Jima had "Rodent Exterminator" written on their helmet covers, and on one American flagship the naval commander had erected a large sign enjoining all to "KILL JAPS! KILL JAPS! KILL MORE JAPS!" . . . Why not, indeed, drop a new kind of bomb on them, and on the un-uniformed ones too, since the Japanese government has announced that women from ages of seventeen to forty are being called up to repel the invasion? The intelligence officer of the U.S. Fifth Air Force declared on July 21, 1945, that "the entire population of Japan is a proper military target," and he added emphatically, *"There are no civilians in Japan."* Why delay and allow one more American high school kid to see his own intestines blown out of his body and spread before him in the dirt while he screams and screams when with the new bomb we can end the whole thing just like that? . . .

No Cause for Shame

When the *Enola Gay* dropped its package, "There were cheers," says [historian] John Toland, "over the intercom; it meant the end of the war." Down on the ground the reaction of Sledge's marine buddies when they heard the news was more solemn and complicated. They heard about the end of the war

> with quiet disbelief coupled with an indescribable sense of relief. We thought the Japanese would never surrender. Many refused to believe it. . . . Sitting in stunned silence, we remembered our dead. So many dead. So many maimed. So many bright futures consigned to the ashes of the past. So many dreams lost in the madness that had engulfed us. Except for a few widely scattered shouts of joy, the survivors of the abyss sat hollow-eyed and silent, trying to comprehend a world without war.

These troops who cried and cheered with relief or who sat stunned by the weight of their experience are very different from the high-minded, guilt-ridden GIs we're told about by J. Glenn Gray in his sensitive book *The Warriors.* . . . Glenn Gray was not in a rifle company, or even just behind one. "When the news of the atomic bombing of Hiroshima and Nagasaki came," he asks us to believe, "many an American soldier felt shocked and ashamed." Shocked, OK, but why ashamed? Because we'd destroyed civilians? We'd been doing that for years, in raids on Hamburg and Berlin and Cologne and Frankfurt and Mannheim and Dresden, and Tokyo, and besides, the two A-bombs wiped out 10,000 Japanese troops, not often thought of now, [author] John Hersey's kindly physicians and Jesuit priests being more touching. If around division headquarters some of the people Gray talked to felt ashamed, down in the rifle companies no one did, despite Gray's assertions. "The combat soldier," he says,

> "The purpose of the bombs was not to 'punish' people but to stop the war."

> knew better than did Americans at home what those bombs meant in suffering and injustice. The man of conscience realized intuitively that the vast majority of Japanese in both cities were no more, if no less, guilty of the war than were his own parents, sisters, or brothers.

I find this canting nonsense. The purpose of the bombs was not to "punish" people but to stop the war. To intensify the shame Gray insists we feel, he seems willing to fiddle the facts. The Hiroshima bomb, he says, was dropped "without any warning." But actually, two days before, 720,000 leaflets were dropped on the city urging everyone to get out and indicating that the place was going to be (as the Potsdam Declaration has promised) obliterated. Of course few left.

Experience whispers that the pity is not that we used the bomb to end the Japanese war but that it wasn't ready in time to end the German one. If only it could have been rushed into production faster and dropped at the right moment . . . , much of the Nazi hierarchy could have been pulverized immediately, saving not just the embarrassment of the Nuremberg trials but the lives of around four million Jews, Poles, Slavs, and gypsies, not to mention the lives and limbs of millions of Allied and German soldiers. If the bomb had only been ready in time, the young men of my infantry platoon would not have been so cruelly killed and wounded.

Two Sides to the Tragedy

All this is not to deny that like the Russian Revolution, the atom-bombing of Japan was a vast historical tragedy, and every passing year magnifies the dilemma into which it has lodged the contemporary world. As with the Russian Revolution, there are two sides—that's why it's a tragedy instead of a disaster—and unless we are . . . simplemindedly unimaginative and cruel, we will be painfully aware of both sides at once.

To observe that from the viewpoint of the war's victims-to-be the bomb seemed precisely the right thing to drop is to purchase no immunity from horror. . . .

> [Truman] knew war, and he knew better than some of his critics then and now what he was doing and why he was doing it.

The stupidity, parochialism, and greed in the international mismanagement of the whole nuclear challenge should not tempt us . . . to infer retrospectively extraordinary corruption, imbecility, or motiveless malignity in those who decided, all things considered, to drop the bomb. Times change. Harry Truman was not a fascist but a democrat. He was as close to a genuine egalitarian as anyone we've seen in high office for a long time. He is the only President in my lifetime who ever had experience in a small unit of ground troops whose mission it was to kill people. That sort of experience of actual war seems useful to presidents especially, helping to inform them about life in general and restraining them from making fools of themselves needlessly. . . .

[Truman] knew war, and he knew better than some of his critics then and now what he was doing and why he was doing it. "Having found the bomb," he said, "we have used it. . . . We have used it to shorten the agony of young Americans."

The past, which as always did not know the future, acted in ways that ask to be imagined before they are condemned. Or even simplified.

Many Scientists Who Worked on the A-Bomb Opposed Its Use

Leo Szilard

In the following interview, Leo Szilard, one of the foremost scientists who worked on the atomic bomb, says that he strongly opposed its use. He feels that US President Harry S. Truman and his advisers did not understand the issues and failed to give enough attention to alternatives. Although Japan would not have surrendered unconditionally without the use of military force, he says, if terms like those actually given after the surrender had been offered, there could have been a negotiated peace treaty. In his opinion, dropping the atomic bomb set a bad precedent that precipitated the nuclear arms race. Szilard was a Hungarian-born physicist who helped persuade President Franklin D. Roosevelt to launch the atomic bomb project to keep Nazi Germany from getting it first. He had a major role in the bomb's development, but later led opposition to its use against Japan.

SOURCE. Leo Szilard, "President Truman Did Not Understand," *U.S. News & World Report*, 1960. Reproduced by permission.

Interviewer: *Dr. Szilard, what was your attitude in 1945 toward the question of dropping the atomic bomb in Japan?*

Leo Szilard: I opposed it with all my power, but I'm afraid not as effectively as I should have wished.

Did any other scientists feel the same way you did?

Very many other scientists felt this way. This is particularly true of Oak Ridge and the Metallurgical Laboratory of the University of Chicago. I don't know how the scientists felt at Los Alamos.

At the Oak Ridge and Chicago branches of the A-bomb project, was there any division of opinion?

I'll say this: Almost without exception, all the creative physicists had misgivings about the use of the bomb. I would not say the same about the chemists. The biologists felt very much as the physicists did.

When did your misgivings first arise?

Well, I started to worry about the use of the bomb in the spring of '45. But misgivings about our way of conducting ourselves arose in Chicago when we first learned that we were using incendiary bombs on a large scale against the cities of Japan.

This, of course, was none of our responsibility. There was nothing we could do about it, but I do remember that my colleagues in the project were disturbed about it.

Did you have any knowledge of Secretary of War [Henry] Stimson's concern at this time on the question of using the bomb?

I knew that Mr. Stimson was a thoughtful man who gave the bomb serious consideration. He was one of the most thoughtful members of the [President Harry] Truman cabinet. However, I certainly have to take exception to the article Stimson wrote after Hiroshima in *Harper's Magazine*. He wrote that a "demonstration" of

> Almost without exception, all the creative physicists had misgivings about the use of the bomb.

the A-bomb was impossible because we had only two bombs. Had we staged a "demonstration," both bombs might have been duds and then we would have lost face.

Now, this argument is clearly invalid. It is quite true that at the time of Hiroshima we had only two bombs, but it would not have been necessary to wait for very long before we would have had several more.

Were you aware then of the attitude of Under Secretary of the Navy Ralph Bard or of the memorandum by [naval officer] Lewis L. Strauss?

No.

So, in effect, there was no concerted opposition to military use of the bomb?

No, there was none. You see, it would have been impossible for me to go and talk with Lewis Strauss because of the secrecy rules.

> There was no need to demand the unconditional surrender of Japan.

Do you feel that President Truman and those immediately below him gave full and conscientious study to all the alternatives to [the] use of the atomic bomb?

I do not think they did. They thought only in terms of our having to end the war by military means.

I don't think Japan would have surrendered unconditionally without the use of force. But there was no need to demand the unconditional surrender of Japan. If we had offered Japan the kind of peace treaty which we actually gave her, we could have had a negotiated peace.

Petition to the President

In retrospect, do you think your views got a full hearing? . . .

[After attempts to reach first President Franklin Roosevelt and then President Truman] I drafted a petition to the President which did not go into any considerations of expediency but opposed, on purely moral grounds,

Physicist Leo Szilard believed many of his colleagues, scientists instrumental in making the atomic bomb, felt as he did that its wartime use was wrong. (Time & Life Pictures/Getty Images.)

the use of atomic bombs against the cities of Japan. This petition was signed by about 60 members of the Chicago project. Some of those who signed insisted that the petition be transmitted to the President through "official channels." To this I reluctantly agreed. I was, at this point, mainly concerned that the members of the project had an opportunity to go on record on this issue, and I didn't think that the petition would be likely to have an effect on the course of events. The petition was sent to the President through official channels, and I should not be too surprised if it were discovered one of these days that it hadn't ever reached him.

Did you think then that the Russians probably were working on the bomb?

I had no idea of this. The question before us was: Should we think in terms of America's having a long-term monopoly of the bomb after the war, or will Russia have the bomb before long also? I had no doubt that we would start an atomic-arms race if we used the bomb.

Would a demonstration have been feasible?

It is easy to see, at least in retrospect, how an effective demonstration could have been staged. We could have communicated with Japan through regular diplomatic channels—say, through Switzerland—and explained to the Japanese that we didn't want to kill anybody, and therefore proposed that one city—say, Hiroshima—be evacuated. Then one single bomber would come and drop one single bomb.

But again, I don't believe this staging a demonstration was the real issue, and in a sense it is just as immoral to force a sudden ending of a war by threatening violence as by using violence. My point is that violence would not have been necessary if we had been willing to negotiate. After all, Japan was suing for peace.

Did you know that fully at the time?

No. All I knew at that time was that we had won the war, that Japan had not the ghost of a chance of winning it and that she must know this. It did not matter just how far gone the Japanese were; if they knew they would not win the war, if they knew they would lose it in the end, that is all that matters.

The Major Mistake

Have your views on this subject changed at all since 1945?

No, except that I can say much more clearly today what I was thinking at that time than I was able to say it at that time. Today I would put the whole emphasis on the mistake of insisting on unconditional surrender. Today I would say that the confusion arose from considering the fake alternatives of either having to invade Japan or of having to use the bomb against her cities.

> The confusion arose from considering the fake alternatives of either having to invade Japan or of having to use the bomb against her cities.

Would most other nations, including Russia, have done the same thing we did, confronted with the same opportunity to use the bomb?

Look, answering this question would be pure speculation. I can say this, however: By and large, governments are guided by considerations of expediency rather than by moral considerations. And this, I think, is a universal law of how governments act.

Prior to the war I had the illusion that up to a point the American Government was different. This illusion was gone after Hiroshima.

Perhaps you remember that in 1939 President Roosevelt warned the belligerents against using bombs against the inhabited cities, and this I thought was perfectly fitting and natural.

Then, during the war, without any explanation, we began to use incendiary bombs against the cities of Japan. This was disturbing to me and it was disturbing many of my friends.

Was that the end of the illusion?

Yes, this was the end of the illusion. But, you see, there was still a difference between using incendiary bombs and using the new force of nature for purposes of destruction. There was still a further step taken here— atomic energy was something new.

I thought it would be very bad to set a precedent for using atomic energy for purposes of destruction. And I think that having done so we have greatly affected the postwar history.

How Bombing Boomeranged

In what way?

I think it made it very difficult for us to take the position after the war that we wanted to get rid of atomic bombs because it would be immoral to use them against the civilian population. We lost the moral argument with which, right after the war, we might have perhaps gotten rid of the bomb.

Let me say only this much to the moral issue involved: Suppose Germany had developed two bombs before we had any bombs. And suppose Germany had dropped one bomb, say, on Rochester and the other on Buffalo, and then having run out of bombs she would have lost the war. Can anyone doubt that we would then have defined the dropping of atomic bombs on cities as a war crime, and that we would have sentenced the Germans who were guilty of this crime to death at Nuremberg and hanged them?

But, again, don't misunderstand me. The only conclusion we can draw is that governments acting in a crisis are guided by questions of expediency, and moral considerations are given very little weight, and that America is no different from any other nation in this respect.

How would the world of today have been different if we had not dropped the atomic bomb on Japan?

I think, if we had not dropped the bomb on Hiroshima and instead demonstrated the bomb after the war, then, if we had really wanted to rid the world of atomic bombs, I think we could probably have done it.

Now, whether this would have led to a better world or not, I don't know. But it certainly would have been a world very different from the one we have now.

Do you think it would have avoided a nuclear-arms race?

I think we could have avoided a nuclear-arms race, yes, but we might still have gotten into conflict with Russia—over other issues.

Would the Russians have developed the atomic and hydrogen bombs as quickly if we had not dropped the bomb? Do you think they hurried up their espionage and research after Hiroshima?

They had no choice but to hurry up with developing their own bomb, since they would not want us to have the monopoly of the bomb.

Were the Russians aware of the work we were doing?

Yes. This I did not know at the time. I would say, in retrospect, that not testing the bomb probably would not have gained us very much time.

Do you think that the "missile age" would have come as quickly without the atomic bomb?

No, the long-range missile would be completely useless without a nuclear warhead, because they are too expensive as vehicles for carrying TNT.

What about the space age in general? Would that also have been put off into the indefinite future?

I should think so.

Then was space exploration—missile, hydrogen bombs, all the rest of it—a natural outgrowth of the atomic bomb?

I think so. But, you see, I'm in no hurry to get to Mars or Venus. I don't value the exploration of the solar system as much as maybe others do.

How the Bomb Affected Americans

Do Americans have a guilt complex over the bomb?

I wouldn't call it exactly a "guilt complex." But you remember perhaps John Hersey's [lengthy 1946 article in the *New Yorker*] "Hiroshima." It made a very great impression on America, but it did not in England. Why?

It was we who used the bomb and not the English. Somewhere, below the level of consciousness, we have a

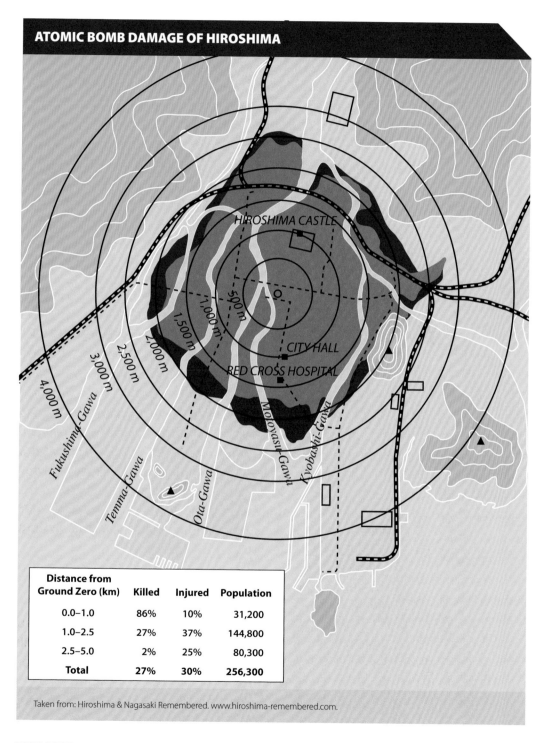

ATOMIC BOMB DAMAGE OF HIROSHIMA

HIROSHIMA CASTLE

500 m
1,000 m
1,500 m
2,000 m
2,500 m
3,000 m
4,000 m

CITY HALL
RED CROSS HOSPITAL

Fukushima-Gawa
Temma-Gawa
Ota-Gawa
Motoyasu-Gawa
Kyobashi-Gawa

Distance from Ground Zero (km)	Killed	Injured	Population
0.0–1.0	86%	10%	31,200
1.0–2.5	27%	37%	144,800
2.5–5.0	2%	25%	80,300
Total	**27%**	**30%**	**256,300**

Taken from: Hiroshima & Nagasaki Remembered. www.hiroshima-remembered.com.

> Great power imposes the obligation of exercising restraint, and we did not live up to this obligation.

stake in the bomb, which the English don't have. Still, I wouldn't call it a "guilt complex."

Has this feeling, whatever it is, affected us in any material way?

Great power imposes the obligation of exercising restraint, and we did not live up to this obligation. I think this affected many of the scientists in a subtle sense, and it diminished their desire to continue to work on the bomb.

Did Hiroshima affect our development of the hydrogen bomb?

I should say it delayed it five years. I think, if we'd exercised restraint, many physicists would have continued to work on atomic energy after the war who did not.

Would a United States Government today, confronted with the same set of choices and approximately the same degree of military intelligence, reach a different decision as to using the first A-bomb?

I think it depends on the person of the President. Truman did not understand what was involved. You can see that from the language he used. Truman announced the bombing of Hiroshima while he was at sea coming back from Potsdam, and his announcement contained the phrase—I quote from the *New York Times* of August 7, 1945: "We have spent 2 billion dollars on the greatest scientific gamble in history—and won."

To put the atomic bomb in terms of having gambled 2 billion dollars and having "won" offended my sense of proportions, and I concluded at that time that Truman did not understand at all what was involved.

The Decision to Use the Atomic Bomb Seemed Right at the Time

Max Hastings

In the following viewpoint, Max Hastings, writing on the sixtieth anniversary of the dropping of the first atomic bombs, contends that despite what is said by those who regard the bombings as war crimes, there is plenty of evidence that Japan was preparing for a sacrificial defense that would have cost many lives had there been an invasion. On the other hand, there is also evidence that Japan was defeated and wanted to end the war. US leaders of that time could not be sure what Japan would do and were already conducting conventional bombing raids that killed more people than the atomic bombs. Although President Harry Truman's decision may seem questionable now, there are good reasons why it seemed right at the time. Hastings is a British journalist, editor, and historian. He is the author of *Retribution: The Battle for Japan, 1944–45* and many other books about military history.

SOURCE. Max Hastings, "What Would You Have Done?" *Manchester Guardian*, 2005. Reproduced by permission of the author.

The 60th anniversary of the dropping of the first atomic bomb falls a week [from] today [on August 6, 2005]. The occasion will be marked by a torrent of prose from those who regard the destruction of Hiroshima and of Nagasaki three days later as "war crimes," forever attaching shame to those who ordered them. By contrast, there will be a plethora of dismissive comment from pundits who believe the nuclear assault saved a million allied casualties in 1945, by causing Japan to surrender without an invasion of its mainland.

Plentiful evidence is available to both schools. In the spring of 1945, Americans fighting in the Pacific were awed by the suicidal resistance they encountered. Hundreds of Japanese pilots, thousands of soldiers and civilians, immolated themselves, inflicting heavy US losses, rather than accept the logic of surrender.

Japan Was Planning Sacrificial Defense Against Invasion

It was well-known that the Japanese forces were preparing a similar sacrificial defence of their homeland. Allied planning for an invasion in the autumn of 1945 assumed hundreds of thousands of casualties. Allied soldiers—and prisoners—in the far east were profoundly grateful when the atomic bombs, in their eyes, saved their lives.

On the other side of the argument is the fact that in the summer of 1945 Japan's economy was collapsing. The US submarine blockade had strangled oil and raw-materials supply lines. Air attack had destroyed many factories, and 60% of civilian housing. Some authoritative Washington analysts asserted that Japan's morale was cracking.

Intercepts of Japanese diplomatic cables revealed to Washington that Tokyo was soliciting [Soviet premier Joseph] Stalin's good offices to end the war. The Americans were also aware of the Soviets' imminent intention

Photo on following page: Japanese soldiers sometimes killed themselves rather than surrender to American troops. (Getty Images.)

to invade Japanese-occupied China in overwhelming strength.

In short, the 2005 evidence demonstrates that Japan had no chance of sustaining effective resistance. If America's fleets had merely lingered offshore through autumn 1945, they could have watched the Japanese people, already desperately hungry, starve to death or perish beneath conventional bombing. Oddly enough, Soviet entry into the war on August 8 was more influential than the atomic explosions in convincing Japanese leaders that they must quit.

In some eyes, this adds up to a devastating indictment against President Harry Truman, who launched the most murderous weapon in history against a nation already doomed. How is it possible, in the light of such facts, for students like me to retain sympathy—enthusiasm is impossible—for Truman's decision?

The foremost answer is that much we now know was then uncertain. Amid their defeats in 1941–42, the allies had developed an exaggerated respect for their enemy's might. They did not comprehend in 1945 how close was Japan's industrial collapse.

The Leadership of Japan Was Divided

Second, although Tokyo plainly wanted to escape from the war, its terms remained confused. There is little doubt that if Washington had explicitly promised that the emperor [Hirohito] might retain his throne, Japan would have bowed. But so faltering and divided was Japan's leadership that the US still possessed grounds for real doubt about Tokyo's intentions. And why should Washington offer guarantees for Hirohito's future when he had been at least the figurehead for Japan's terrible deeds?

> It was not that [Japanese military leaders] deluded themselves that they could win. Rather, they preferred death to humiliation.

Many Japanese generals bitterly opposed surrender even after the Soviet invasion, Hiroshima and Nagasaki. It was not that they deluded themselves that they could win. Rather, they preferred death to humiliation.

All wars brutalise all participants, but both sides in the Pacific had become exceptionally desensitised. The great war correspondent Ernie Pyle wrote shortly before his own death in combat: "In Europe we felt that our enemies, horrible and deadly as they were, were still people. But out here I soon gathered that the Japanese were looked upon as something subhuman and repulsive, the way people feel about cockroaches and mice."

Japan's occupation of China had cost 15 million Chinese lives. Civilians had been raped, tortured, enslaved and massacred, while British and US prisoners were subjected to hideous maltreatment. The Japanese had been waging biological warfare in China. Their notorious Unit 731 subjected hundreds of prisoners to vivisection [cutting or surgery for medical experimentation on living beings]. Many captured American airmen were beheaded. Some were eaten. A B-29 crew was dissected alive at a Japanese city hospital.

> More people—100,000—died in the March 9 Tokyo incendiary attack than at Hiroshima.

Americans, in their turn, showed themselves reluctant to take prisoners. They subjected Japan's cities to the vast fire-bombing raids which began in March 1945, killing half a million people. [Historians] Lawrence Freedman and Saki Dockrill, in a powerful analysis, argue that the nuclear assault must be perceived in the context of the deadly incendiary raids that preceded it: "Nobody involved in the decision on the atomic bombs could have seen themselves as setting new precedents for mass destruction in scale—only in efficiency." More people—100,000—died in the March 9 Tokyo incendiary attack than at Hiroshima.

The Japanese Surrender

Following the bombing of Hiroshima on August 6, 1945, the Japanese government met to consider what to do next. The emperor had been urging since June that Japan find some way to end the war, but the Japanese Minister of War and the heads of both the Army and the Navy . . . hoped that if they could hold out until the ground invasion of Japan began, they would be able to inflict so many casualties on the Allies that Japan still might win some sort of negotiated settlement. . . .

[After] the Soviet declaration of war on Japan of August 8, 1945, and the atomic bombing of Nagasaki of the following day, another Imperial Council was held the night of August 9–10, and this time the vote on surrender was a tie, 3-to-3. For the first time in a generation, the emperor stepped forward from his normally ceremonial-only role and personally broke the tie, ordering Japan to surrender. . . .

Debate raged within the Japanese government over whether to accept the American terms or fight on. Meanwhile, American leaders were growing impatient, and on August 13 conventional air raids resumed on Japan. Thousands more Japanese civilians died while their leaders delayed. The Japanese people learned of the surrender negotiations for the first time when, on August 14, B-29s showered Tokyo with thousands of leaflets. . . . Later that day, the

The Atomic Bombs Set No Precedent for Destruction

We may dismiss conspiracy theories that Hiroshima was a first shot in the cold war, designed to impress the Soviets. Rather, the use of a "total" weapon reflected the inexorable logic of total war.

Amid a conflict in which 50 million people had already died, those who dispatched the *Enola Gay* viewed the judgment with gravity, but without the sense of uniqueness that posterity perceives as appropriate. Uncertainty persisted in August 1945 about whether the bombs would work.

This was one reason for Washington's reluctance to stage an offshore demonstration, though more potent was emperor called another meeting of his cabinet and instructed them to accept the Allied terms immediately, explaining, "I cannot endure the thought of letting my people suffer any longer"; if the war did not end "the whole nation would be reduced to ashes." . . .

Loyalty to the emperor was an absolute in the Japanese military, but so was the refusal to surrender, and now that the two had come into conflict, open rebellion was a possible result. The emperor recorded a message in which he personally accepted the Allied surrender terms. . . . This way everyone in Japan would know that surrender was the emperor's personal will. Some within the Japanese military actually attempted to steal this recording before it could be broadcast, while others attempted a more general military coup in order to seize power and continue the war.

On August 15, 1945, the emperor's broadcast announcing Japan's surrender was heard via radio all over Japan. For most of his subjects, it was the first time that they had ever heard his voice.

SOURCE. *"Japan Surrenders (August 10–15, 1945)," The Manhattan Project: An Interactive History, US Department of Energy Office of History and Heritage Resources. www.cfo.doe.gov/me70/ manhattan.*

a desire to administer to the enemy a devastating shock, such as only city attacks were thought able to achieve.

The decision-makers were men who had grown accustomed to the necessity for cruel judgments. There was overwhelming technological momentum: a titanic effort had been made to create a weapon for which the allies saw themselves as competing with their foes.

After Hiroshima, General Leslie Groves, chief of the Manhattan Project, was almost the only man to succumb to triumphalism. He said: "We have spent $21 billion on the greatest scientific gamble in history—we won."[1] Having devoted such resources to the bomb, an extraordinary initiative would have been needed from Truman to arrest its employment.

Those who today find it easy to condemn the architects of Hiroshima sometimes seem to lack humility in recognising the frailties of the decision-makers, mortal men grappling with dilemmas of a magnitude our own generation has been spared.

In August 1945, amid a world sick of death in the cause of defeating evil, allied lives seemed very precious, while the enemy appeared to value neither his own nor those of the innocent. Truman's Hiroshima judgment may seem wrong in the eyes of posterity, but it is easy to understand why it seemed right to most of his contemporaries.

Note

1. This quote is actually attributed to President Harry Truman.

The Atomic Bombing of Japan Prevented a Third World War

Klaus Wiegrefe

In the following viewpoint, written for a European audience, Klaus Wiegrefe declares that the atomic bombing of Hiroshima and Nagasaki put an end to the spiral of increasing destruction in war because it forced the superpowers to seek peaceful solutions to their disputes. In particular, he says, postwar Germany benefited from it because the memory of Hiroshima caused relations between West and East Germany to be stable during the Cold War even though the atomic bomb was originally developed for use against Nazi Germany. Wiegrefe heads the history department at *Der Spiegel*, Europe's leading news magazine, which is published in Hamburg, Germany. This article was translated from German for its international website.

SOURCE. Klaus Wiegrefe, "Remembering Hiroshima Parts 1 and 2," *Der Spiegel* (international online edition), Christopher Sultan, 2005. Reproduced by permission.

There were 76,000 houses in Hiroshima [Japan] on the morning of August 6 [1945], and 70,000 were destroyed or damaged by the explosion of a single weapon. The Americans called the deadly monster "Little Boy," because the bomb, three meters long and weighing in at almost five tons, turned out to be substantially smaller than its designers had initially expected. It was the first atom bomb to be used as a weapon in the history of mankind.

The devastation caused by "Little Boy" surpassed everything that American scientists, military personnel and politicians had expected. The nuclear explosion left behind death and destruction within an area of 13 square kilometers, or about five square miles. On August 6, there were about 350,000 people in the city, the country's eighth largest. Most were Japanese, but there were also tens of thousands of Korean and Chinese forced laborers, a few American prisoners of war and at least a dozen German Jesuits who had come to Hiroshima because they felt relatively safe there against US air attacks.

The Atomic Plague

By the end of 1945, about 140,000 of those had died—in horror-inspiring ways. The first victims were essentially vaporized in the epicenter of the fireball, at temperatures of more than a million degrees centigrade, or burned to death in a wave of heat hot enough to scorch trees a dozen kilometers away. Still others were crushed by the debris from buildings collapsing as a result of the massive wave of pressure. Those at a somewhat greater distance from ground zero were killed by direct exposure to radiation. Many were poisoned when they drank the radioactive rain—turned black by dust and debris—that began falling about 20 minutes after the explosion. An Australian journalist visiting Hiroshima in September 1945 dubbed the disease he observed—hair falling out, bodies covered in reddish-purple spots, victims dying of internal bleeding—the "atomic plague."

Three days after the inferno, the Americans dropped a second bomb—"Fat Man"—on Nagasaki, almost completely destroying the venerable commercial city.

The exact number of victims of Hiroshima and Nagasaki will never be known. What we do know is that thousands are still dying today from the delayed effects of malicious radiation. It's almost as if the punishment pronounced in the Second Commandment of the Old Testament, that of a jealous God punishing the unfaithful "to the third and the fourth generation," had been meted out by human hands. Even the children and grandchildren of the survivors of Hiroshima and Nagasaki will suffer the consequences of their parents' and grandparents' exposure to radiation. In many cases, their genetic material has been so severely damaged that they now suffer from leukemia, breast cancer and neurological disorders.

> "No other military strike changed the history of mankind as much as the dropping of 'Little Boy' and 'Fat Man' on Japan."

The nuclear age began in the ruins of Hiroshima. The enormous destruction that nuclear energy can cause first became evident 60 years ago, in the delta of the Ota River on the southeastern coast of Japan's main island, Honshu. The co-pilot of the B-29 Superfortress that dropped the Hiroshima bomb, Robert A. Lewis, had gazed down on the burning city and watched as a mushroom cloud rose into the sky. He later wrote: "My God, what have we done."

An End to the Spiral of Destruction

No other military strike changed the history of mankind as much as the dropping of "Little Boy" and "Fat Man" on Japan. Until 1945, it was generally believed that advances in weapons technology would lead to exponential increases in the numbers of dead and wounded in a subsequent war. Whether these advances related to gunpowder, bombers, submarines or tanks—progress in the military arena was always synonymous with ever-growing fatality counts and ever-increasing physical devastation.

More than 775,000 soldiers died in Napoleon's military campaigns between 1805 and 1815. One hundred years later, World War I claimed almost 15 million lives. Finally, Hitler's World War II sent 60 million people to their graves, including the victims of Hiroshima and Nagasaki.

> It was the cosmic destructive force of the new nuclear weapons that forced the world's superpowers, for the first time in history, to deal with their rivalries with primarily peaceful means.

But it was the atom bomb, the biggest destructive force known to man, that ultimately put an end to this spiral of death and destruction. It was the cosmic destructive force of the new nuclear weapons that forced the world's superpowers, for the first time in history, to deal with their rivalries with primarily peaceful means. Despite the fact that Soviet communism and Western democracy were diametrically opposed to one another, World War II wasn't followed by a third world war, but by the Cold War, which in fact was—as US historian John Lewis Gaddis calls it—a "long peace."

It was precisely the ability to extinguish one another and, in the future, all of mankind, that deterred the Americans and the Russians from resorting to what US President Harry Truman called the "energy of the sun" to settle their rivalries.

Even the fathers of the Hiroshima bomb were fully conscious of crossing a boundary, and of there being no turning back. In the summer of 1945, US General Leslie Groves, who headed the project that culminated in the atomic bomb, wrote: "We dare tamper with the forces heretofore reserved for the Almighty." Upon witnessing the first atomic test, Groves, the son of a pastor, interpreted the "horrible roar" of the explosion as a "warning of the Last Judgment." . . .

"We Must Act"

Historians have devoted a great deal of thought to the question of why the United States was the first to successfully build an atomic bomb. After all, in 1939 the United States is far behind other countries when it comes to military prowess. Most of its weapons and tanks are vintage World War I, and its relatively small armed forces are ranked only 17th in the world.

But the president sitting in the White House at the time reacts with vision and decisiveness. [Franklin] Roosevelt meets twice with one of [Albert] Einstein's emissaries, who is sent to Washington to explain the science behind atomic energy to the president.

In the first meeting, the president has trouble understanding what the scientists are talking about. But in the second meeting, on October 12, 1939, he finally comprehends the enormity of their warnings. "What you are saying," he tells the scientists, "is that you want to make sure that the Nazis don't blow us up." "Exactly," the emissary says, to which Roosevelt responds: "Then we must act." . . .

The "Manhattan Project," named after the pioneering "Manhattan District of Engineers" of the US Army Corps of Engineers, becomes what is until then the biggest armaments project in the history of mankind.

The US Army purchases or seizes large tracts of land in the states of Washington, Tennessee and New Mexico. Soon, 125,000 people, including six current or future Noble laureates, are working in the 37 major facilities of the country's top-secret atomic weapons program.

In 1943, the country's top scientists, half of them European emigrants, leave their posts at preeminent universities like the University of California at Berkeley and at the University of Chicago to settle on a barren high desert plateau in New Mexico's thinly populated Los Alamos region. . . . The remote location is chosen to make it easier for the US counterintelligence agency, the CIC, to conceal the project from Hitler's spies.

Within a few months, a small city of apartment buildings and prefabricated homes develops in the high desert of New Mexico, about 6,500 feet above sea level. Armed guards patrol a 10-foot barbed-wire fence surrounding the so-called technical area where laboratories and production buildings are housed. An alarm system detects any movement along the fence, while spotlights keep the area brightly lit at night. The CIC starts a rumor in the surrounding area that the facility is a hospital for pregnant US Army wives, which explains the plethora of doctors.

The military head of the project, Groves, whom President Roosevelt has instructed to maintain "absolute secrecy," has his agents tap the scientists' telephone conversations. The Americans, who are considering a plan to kidnap Hitler's top scientist, [Werner] Heisenberg, fear that their German adversaries could be hatching similar plans, and the program's leading experts are constantly accompanied by bodyguards whenever they leave the Los Alamos facility.

A Bomb Too Secret to Drop on Germany

The only allies Roosevelt entrusts with the secret project are the British. The two countries' physicists operate hand-in-hand, and London carries a portion of the costs. In 1943, the US president and British Prime Minister Winston Churchill agree not to "use the atom bomb against third parties without the other's consent." In keeping with the agreement, Churchill later consents to the Hiroshima and Nagasaki bombings. . . .

The emigre scientists from Germany have no idea that the fruits of their research are no longer intended for an explosion over the Third Reich. One of the most astonishing finds in recent years is a document containing the minutes of a May 5, 1943, meeting of the high-ranking Military Policy Committee, whose members decided that dropping the atomic bomb over Germany would be too risky. The explosive device could turn out to be a dud, thereby unintentionally providing the Nazis with valuable information to use in developing their own bomb.

Fear of the German bomb has prompted the Americans to build their own. But instead of Germany, they set their sights on Hitler's ally in Asia. . . .

> " Many US strategists view the dropping of an atom bomb as merely an extension of conventional warfare, even though they already sense the new weapon's destructive potential. "

Is it revenge for Pearl Harbor and Japan's brutal methods of waging war in the Pacific? Or does the new US President Harry Truman, who succeeded Roosevelt when he died on April 12, 1945, want to force an end to the war at any price, a war that has already cost the lives of so many GIs? Or is the bomb intended to intimidate Truman's future adversary, Soviet dictator Joseph Stalin?

Many US strategists view the dropping of an atom bomb as merely an extension of conventional warfare, even though they already sense the new weapon's destructive potential. Chief scientist Robert Oppenheimer expects about 20,000 dead in Hiroshima. By comparison, the US Air Force's March 1945 firebombing of Tokyo— a city then consisting mainly of wooden structures— claims about 100,000 lives. . . .

The Truman administration sees the bomb as a tool to reinforce a Pax Americana [American peace] worldwide. Secretary of State [James F.] Byrnes rejects a proposal to share the atomic secret with Stalin, saying: "If we inform the Russians, Stalin will want to be part of it."

In contrast to [Hungarian-born physicist Leo] Szilard, most Los Alamos researchers are in favor of using the bomb. Polish [born] scientist Joseph Rotblat later offers this explanation for his colleagues' behavior: "It was just plain curiosity. They wanted to know if their theoretical calculations and predictions would come to fruition." Rotblat leaves the Manhattan Project when he discovers that the bomb's new target is Japan, not Hitler's Germany. . . .

Truman despises the Japanese, calling them "savages, ruthless, merciless and fanatic." Nevertheless, he instructs Secretary of War Henry Stimson to "only seek out military targets, soldiers and sailors, not women and children." He either doesn't know or refuses to admit that a bomb with the explosive force of about 15,000 tons of TNT will completely destroy an entire city. . . .

The Hiroshima Decision

Truman later justifies the dropping of the atom bombs by citing how many victims a landing in Japan would have claimed, and that his decision "saved the lives of half a million of our boys." In the spring of 1945, the Americans and the Japanese fight one of the bloodiest battles of World War II on the island of Okinawa. About 50,000 GIs—almost a third of US forces deployed in the campaign—are killed or wounded. Truman wants to make sure that a massacre of such proportions will never be repeated.

> [The Japanese] order their troops to engage in hand-to-hand combat in the event of an invasion and, if necessary, to kill women, children and the elderly and use the corpses as shields.

Scientists disagree, citing the US military's casualty projections from 1945, which are substantially lower. But even Truman's critics refuse to question the president's deep concern for the fate of the "boys." "Think of all the kids who won't be killed now. That's the most important thing," the man in the White House, clearly pleased, writes to his wife when Kremlin dictator Stalin indicates that he will comply with America's wishes and attack Japan in August 1945, a move that would significantly improve the prospects of a swift end to the war.

Does Truman have any alternatives to using the atom bomb? A naval blockade, for instance? The Japanese fleet has been destroyed, the country's weakened air defenses pose only a minor risk to US bombers, the weapons industry is in ruins, and the Japanese people are starving. Food shortages and outbreaks of disease would likely force Tokyo to capitulate by year's end.

Of course, many more Japanese would die in an invasion—experts say a million—than were killed in Hiroshima and Nagasaki.

But, more importantly, an invasion scenario would run straight against the strengthening tide of public opinion. Japan's war cost 15 million Chinese, Koreans, Britons, Americans and Filipinos their lives in the Pacific theater and the American public wants a quick end to the war. No president would have been able to refrain from using a weapon on the grounds that it would save Japanese lives. . . .

In the spring and summer of 1945, after US intelligence cracks the Japanese code, the Americans are able to intercept and read telegrams sent by the foreign ministry in Tokyo to the Japanese embassy in Moscow. The exchanges suggest to Truman that there is a small but growing number of officials and politicians in the Japanese imperial government who would consider ending the war. But Nippon's powerful military leaders reject all overtures, still hoping for victory or at least a conditional peace that will enable them to retain their power. They order their troops to engage in hand-to-hand combat in the event of an invasion and, if necessary, to kill women, children and the elderly and use the corpses as shields. . . .

On July 26, 1945, the Western powers give the administration in Tokyo a choice: risk "total devastation" of the country or surrender unconditionally. Truman notes in his diary: "I am certain that they will not do it, but we must give them the chance."

Truman's hunch proves to be correct. At a press conference, Japanese Prime Minister Kantaro Suzuki announces that the Allied proposal is untrustworthy, and that "for this reason we will ignore it."

Was the Atomic Bomb Necessary?

There has been much dispute over whether Truman, with his unwillingness to compromise, lost the opportunity to achieve victory without resorting to the atom bomb. After all, the offer of capitulation while preserving the monarchy would have strengthened the position of those in favor of peace in Tokyo. . . .

The fact that it took dropping a second atom bomb over Nagasaki in August, as well as the Soviet invasion of Japan, to convince [Emperor] Hirohito to stand up to his military leaders reinforces doubts that an offer of compromise from Potsdam one month earlier would have been very effective.

Just before the conference is set to begin in the former Cecilienhof Palace in Potsdam, Truman still doesn't know whether the atom bomb will work.

The first test in New Mexico's Alamogordo Desert is planned for July 16. That evening, Secretary of War Stimson receives telegram number 32,887 at his villa in a Berlin suburb: "Operated on this morning. Diagnosis not yet complete but results seem satisfactory and already exceed expectations." . . .

When US military officials inform their president that the first bomb can be dropped earlier than expected—by early August—the American commander-in-chief is "very excited." On July 31, 1945, he gives the following order: "Release when ready."

Should Truman have waited? Wouldn't the Japanese capitulation have fallen into his lap if he had simply waited for the Soviets to attack, as Stalin had already promised?

All leading Japan experts agree that Moscow's behavior is tremendously important to Tokyo. Even the most narrow-minded Japanese generals know that if they are invaded by the Red Army, they can no longer expect even a negotiated peace. In this respect, it is not just the Americans who are threatening the existence of the royal family. And it's also clear that the emperor, if attacked by the Red Army, will prefer to surrender to Washington—which is precisely what happens.

Despite having the Soviet nuclear arsenal behind them, East German soldiers never fired a shot as the Berlin Wall fell and the Cold War ended. (Getty Images.)

Truman is well aware of the ramifications. Writing in his diary about the possibility of the Soviets entering the war in Asia, Truman notes: "Fini Japs"—the end of the Japanese. Of course, the US president would have had to give his ally, Stalin, the right to participate in the US decision, which is something the American wants to avoid at all costs: "I was not willing to hand over to the Russians the fruits of a long and bitter and courageous fight, a fight in which they had not participated."

> "Since those fateful days in early August 1945, the inhabitants of Hiroshima and Nagasaki have been considered by many as Adolf Hitler's last victims."

To impress Stalin with the super-bomb, Truman lets his opponent in on his plans while still in Potsdam. On the evening of July 24, following a plenary session in the ballroom at Cecilienhof, he tells Stalin, somewhat cryptically, that the Americans have "a new weapon of unusual destructive force." The Soviet premier reacts as if he were pleased, and advises the Americans to "make good use" of the explosive device. The phrase "atom bomb" is never used.

Truman is surprised that the dictator shows so little interest. But, as it turns out, Stalin already knows about the American bomb. A number of scientists who sympathize with the communist anti-fascists in Moscow have already leaked information about the Manhattan Project to Soviet intelligence. Top spy Klaus Fuchs, a communist who has emigrated from Berlin, even took part in the Americans' first test of the bomb in New Mexico. Indeed, Stalin has been pursuing his own atom bomb project for some time prior to the Potsdam Conference. . . .

The Flight of the Enola Gay

In early August, US Colonel [Paul] Tibbets, a member of the special force assembled for the mission, waits on the South Pacific island of Tinian for a typhoon raging in southern Japan to move out to sea. Tibbets is determined to pilot the plane himself, and he names the aircraft "Enola Gay," after his mother.

Tibbets and his team of about 80 men are forced to wait patiently in their barracks for five days—until August 6, 1945—when, at 1:45 A.M. Japanese time, the mission begins. . . .

At 7:25 A.M., the weather scout over Hiroshima transmits the following decisive report: "Cloud cover less than three-tenths at all flying altitudes." At 8:15 A.M., "Little Boy" detonates about 600 meters above what is today the Otemachi parking lot No. 3 at Shima Hospital. A hospital also stood on the same spot in 1945. The building is completely destroyed, the patients vaporized.

Earlier, Truman had noted that the new weapon "may bring about the conflagration that was prophesied in the era of the Euphrates Valley, after Noah and his legendary Ark." And that was precisely what happened.

Since those fateful days in early August 1945, the inhabitants of Hiroshima and Nagasaki have been considered by many as Adolf Hitler's last victims. Without the Nazis' rise to political power in Germany, the Szilards . . . and Einsteins would not have emigrated. Without Hitler, the Americans would never have built the bomb. And if the war in Europe hadn't ended in May 1945, Tibbets' "Little Boy" would probably have been dropped on Berlin, Hamburg or Munich.

It is one of the paradoxical twists of world history that the Germans were able to benefit, only a few years later, from the existence of those weapons that were originally intended for the "Third Reich." Because of the memory of Hiroshima, the border between West and East Germany became one of the most stable segments of the Cold War front—until, in 1989, East Germans took to the streets and brought down the ruling SED, or Socialist Unity Party.

On the day the Berlin Wall came down, more than 1.2 million NATO and Warsaw Pact troops stood facing one another along the entire border between the two Germanys, from Flensburg in the north to Berchtesgaden in the south. Tens of thousands of nuclear weapons, together millions of times more powerful than the Hiroshima bomb, could have destroyed the entire world, and certainly Germany.

But not a single shot was fired.

That, too, is part of the legacy of Hiroshima.

The Atomic Bombing of Japan Was Not Necessary

Mark Weber

In the following viewpoint, Mark Weber argues that the atomic bombings of Hiroshima and Nagasaki were not necessary to end the war because the Japanese were already defeated and US leaders knew they were seeking to negotiate. If the United States had not insisted on unconditional surrender and had made plain that Emperor Hirohito would be allowed to remain in place, he says, Japan would have surrendered immediately. He does not agree with US president Harry S. Truman's claim that the use of the atomic bomb saved many lives. Moreover, leaders such as Generals Dwight Eisenhower and Douglas MacArthur stated that it was not a military necessity. Weber is a historian, lecturer, author, and current affairs analyst. He is the director of the Institute for Historical Review, an independent educational research and publishing center.

SOURCE. Mark Weber, "Was Hiroshima Necessary?" *Journal of Historical Review*, 1997. Reproduced by permission.

On August 6, 1945, the world dramatically entered the atomic age: without either warning or precedent, an American plane dropped a single nuclear bomb on the Japanese city of Hiroshima. The explosion utterly destroyed more than four square miles of the city center. About 90,000 people were killed immediately; another 40,000 were injured, many of whom died in protracted agony from radiation sickness. Three days later, a second atomic strike on the city of Nagasaki killed some 37,000 people and injured another 43,000. Together the two bombs eventually killed an estimated 200,000 Japanese civilians. . . .

> Were the atomic bombings militarily necessary? By any rational yardstick, they were not.

A Beaten Country

Apart from the moral questions involved, were the atomic bombings militarily necessary? By any rational yardstick, they were not. Japan already had been defeated militarily by June 1945. Almost nothing was left of the once mighty Imperial Navy, and Japan's air force had been all but totally destroyed. Against only token opposition, American war planes ranged at will over the country, and US bombers rained down devastation on her cities, steadily reducing them to rubble.

What was left of Japan's factories and workshops struggled fitfully to turn out weapons and other goods from inadequate raw materials. (Oil supplies had not been available since April.) By July about a quarter of all the houses in Japan had been destroyed, and her transportation system was near collapse. Food had become so scarce that most Japanese were subsisting on a sub-starvation diet.

On the night of March 9–10, 1945, a wave of 300 American bombers struck Tokyo, killing 100,000 people. Dropping nearly 1,700 tons of bombs, the war planes ravaged much of the capital city, completely burning out 16 square miles and destroying a quarter of a million structures. A million residents were left homeless.

On May 23, eleven weeks later, came the greatest air raid of the Pacific War, when 520 giant B-29 "Superfortress" bombers unleashed 4,500 tons of incendiary bombs on the heart of the already battered Japanese capital. Generating gale-force winds, the exploding incendiaries obliterated Tokyo's commercial center and railway yards, and consumed the Ginza entertainment district. Two days later, on May 25, a second strike of 502 "Superfortress" planes roared low over Tokyo, raining down some 4,000 tons of explosives. Together these two B-29 raids destroyed 56 square miles of the Japanese capital.

Even before the Hiroshima attack, American air force General Curtis LeMay boasted that American bombers were "driving them [the Japanese] back to the stone age." Henry H. ("Hap") Arnold, commanding General of the Army air forces, declared in his 1949 memoirs: "It always appeared to us, atomic bomb or no atomic bomb, the Japanese were already on the verge of collapse." This was confirmed by former Japanese prime minister Fumimaro Konoye, who said: "Fundamentally, the thing that brought about the determination to make peace was the prolonged bombing by the B-29s."

Japan Seeks Peace

Months before the end of the war, Japan's leaders recognized that defeat was inevitable. . . .

American officials, having long since broken Japan's secret codes, knew from intercepted messages that the country's leaders were seeking to end the war on terms as favorable as possible. Details of these efforts were known from decoded secret communications between the Foreign Ministry in Tokyo and Japanese diplomats abroad. . . .

Emperor Hirohito may have been the only person able to persuade Japan's wartime leadership to surrender. (Getty Images.)

It was only after the war that the American public learned about Japan's efforts to bring the conflict to an end. *Chicago Tribune* reporter Walter Trohan, for example, was obliged by wartime censorship to withhold for seven months one of the most important stories of the war.

In an article that finally appeared August 19, 1945, on the front pages of the *Chicago Tribune* and the *Wash-*

ington Times-Herald, Trohan revealed that on January 20, 1945, two days prior to his departure for the Yalta meeting with [Soviet premier Joseph] Stalin and [British prime minister Winston] Churchill, President Roosevelt received a 40-page memorandum from General Douglas MacArthur outlining five separate surrender overtures from high-level Japanese officials. This memo showed that the Japanese were offering surrender terms virtually identical to the ones ultimately accepted by the Americans at the formal surrender ceremony on September 2— that is, complete surrender of everything but the person of the Emperor. . . .

Is this memorandum authentic? It was supposedly leaked to Trohan by Admiral William D. Leahy, presidential Chief of Staff. Historian Harry Elmer Barnes has related (in "Hiroshima: Assault on a Beaten Foe," *National Review*, May 10, 1958):

> The authenticity of the Trohan article was never challenged by the White House or the State Department, and for very good reason. After General MacArthur returned from Korea in 1951, his neighbor in the Waldorf Towers, former President Herbert Hoover, took the Trohan article to General MacArthur and the latter confirmed its accuracy in every detail and without qualification.

Peace Overtures

In April and May 1945, Japan made three attempts through neutral Sweden and Portugal to bring the war to a peaceful end. . . .

By mid-June, six members of Japan's Supreme War Council had secretly charged Foreign Minister Shigenori Togo with the task of approaching Soviet Russia's leaders "with a view to terminating the war if possible by September." On June 22 the Emperor called a meeting of the Supreme War Council, which included the Prime Minister, the Foreign Minister, and the leading military figures. "We have heard enough of this determination of yours to fight to the last soldiers," said Emperor Hirohito. "We wish that you, leaders of Japan, will strive now to study the ways and the means to conclude the war. In doing so, try not to be bound by the decisions you have made in the past."

By early July the US had intercepted messages from Togo to the Japanese ambassador in Moscow, Naotake Sato, showing that the Emperor himself was taking a personal hand in the peace effort, and had directed that the Soviet Union be asked to help end the war. US officials also knew that the key obstacle to ending the war was American insistence on "unconditional surrender," a demand that precluded any negotiations. The Japanese were willing to accept nearly everything, except turning over their semi-divine Emperor. Heir of a 2,600-year-old dynasty, Hirohito was regarded by his people as a "living god" who personified the nation. (Until the August 15 radio broadcast of his surrender announcement, the Japanese people had never heard his voice.) Japanese particularly feared that the Americans would humiliate the Emperor, and even execute him as a war criminal.

> The Japanese were willing to end the war on any terms, as long as the Emperor was not molested.

On July 12, Hirohito summoned Fumimaro Konoye, who had served as prime minister in 1940–41. Explaining that "it will be necessary to terminate the war without delay," the Emperor said that he wished Konoye to secure peace with the Americans and British through the Soviets. As Prince Konoye later recalled, the Emperor instructed him "to secure peace at any price, notwithstanding its severity." . . .

America's leaders understood Japan's desperate position: the Japanese were willing to end the war on any terms, as long as the Emperor was not molested. If the

US leadership had not insisted on unconditional surrender—that is, if they had made clear a willingness to permit the Emperor to remain in place—the Japanese very likely would have surrendered immediately, thus saving many thousands of lives.

The sad irony is that, as it actually turned out, the American leaders decided anyway to retain the Emperor as a symbol of authority and continuity. They realized, correctly, that Hirohito was useful as a figurehead prop for their own occupation authority in postwar Japan.

Justifications

President Truman steadfastly defended his use of the atomic bomb, claiming that it "saved millions of lives" by bringing the war to a quick end. Justifying his decision, he went so far as to declare: "The world will note that the first atomic bomb was dropped on Hiroshima, a military base. That was because we wished in this first attack to avoid, insofar as possible, the killing of civilians."

This was a preposterous statement. In fact, almost all of the victims were civilians, and the United States Strategic Bombing Survey (issued in 1946) stated in its official report: "Hiroshima and Nagasaki were chosen as targets because of their concentration of activities and population."

If the atomic bomb was dropped to impress the Japanese leaders with the immense destructive power of a new weapon, this could have been accomplished by deploying it on an isolated military base. It was not necessary to destroy a large city. And whatever the justification for the Hiroshima blast, it is much more difficult to defend the second bombing of Nagasaki.

All the same, most Americans accepted, and continue to accept, the official justifications for the bombings. Accustomed to crude propagandistic portrayals of the "Japs" as virtually subhuman beasts, most Americans in 1945 heartily welcomed any new weapon that would wipe out more of the detested Asians, and help avenge the Japanese attack on Pearl Harbor. For the young Americans who were fighting the Japanese in bitter combat, the attitude was "Thank God for the atom bomb." Almost to a man, they were grateful for a weapon whose deployment seemed to end the war and thus allow them to return home.

After the July 1943 firestorm destruction of Hamburg, the mid-February 1945 holocaust of Dresden, and the fire-bombings of Tokyo and other Japanese cities, America's leaders—as US Army General Leslie Groves later commented—"were generally inured to the mass killing of civilians." For President Harry Truman, the killing of tens of thousands of Japanese civilians was simply not a consideration in his decision to use the atom bomb. . . .

> American leaders who were in a position to know the facts did not believe, either at the time or later, that the atomic bombings were needed to end the war.

Authoritative Voices of Dissent

American leaders who were in a position to know the facts did not believe, either at the time or later, that the atomic bombings were needed to end the war.

When he was informed in mid-July 1945 by Secretary of War Henry L. Stimson of the decision to use the atomic bomb, General Dwight Eisenhower was deeply troubled. He disclosed his strong reservations about using the new weapon in his 1963 memoir, *The White House Years: Mandate for Change, 1953–1956*:

During his [Stimson's] recitation of the relevant facts, I had been conscious of a feeling of depression and so I voiced to him my grave misgivings, first on the basis of my belief that Japan was already defeated and that dropping the bomb was completely unnecessary, and secondly because I thought that our country should avoid shocking world opinion by the use of a weapon whose employment was, I thought, no longer mandatory as a measure to save American lives. It was my belief that Japan was, at that very moment, seeking some way to surrender with a minimum loss of "face."

"The Japanese were ready to surrender and it wasn't necessary to hit them with that awful thing . . . I hated to see our country be the first to use such a weapon," Eisenhower said in 1963. . . .

General Douglas MacArthur, Commander of US Army forces in the Pacific, stated on numerous occasions before his death that the atomic bomb was completely unnecessary from a military point of view: "My staff was unanimous in believing that Japan was on the point of collapse and surrender."

General Curtis LeMay, who had pioneered precision bombing of Germany and Japan (and who later headed the Strategic Air Command and served as Air Force chief of staff), put it most succinctly: "The atomic bomb had nothing to do with the end of the war."

The Atomic Bombing of Hiroshima Was Necessary but that of Nagasaki Was Not

Bruce Loebs

In the following viewpoint, Bruce Loebs argues that the atomic bombing of Hiroshima was a necessary evil because without it, the emperor of Japan would not have intervened to dissuade the Japanese military in their determination to keep on fighting. However, he says, there was no justification for the bombing of Nagasaki, as not enough time had passed for the Japanese to surrender. The plan from the beginning was to drop two bombs, and no one in the US government reviewed or challenged it; carrying it through was, in his opinion, a tragic mistake. Loebs is a professor of rhetoric and public address at Idaho State University.

SOURCE. Bruce Loebs, "Hiroshima & Nagasaki: One Necessary Evil, One Tragic Mistake," *Commonweal*, 1995. Reproduced by permission.

America's use of the atomic bomb on Hiroshima and Nagasaki [Japan] fifty years ago [as of 1995] unleashed a debate that has not subsided. Historian Charles Mee damned the use of the atomic bomb as "wanton murder" and Hanson Baldwin, former military editor of the *New York Times*, lamented, "we are now branded with the mark of the beast." In its August 24, 1945, issue *Commonweal* declared: "The name Hiroshima, the name Nagasaki are names for American guilt and shame." Despite such condemnations, a Gallup poll on August 15 [1945] showed that 85 percent of the American people approved "using the new atomic bomb on Japanese cities."

> A Gallup poll on August 15 [1945] showed that 85 percent of the American people approved 'using the new atomic bomb on Japanese cities.'

Today, as then, President [Harry] Truman's defenders agree with Secretary of War Henry Stimson that "this deliberately premeditated destruction was our least abhorrent choice. The destruction of Hiroshima and Nagasaki put an end to the Japanese war. It stopped the fire raids and the strangling blockade; it ended the ghastly specter of a clash of great land armies."

The debate continues in 1995, not only in the academic journals and the mass media but in high-level diplomatic exhanges. President Bill Clinton refused a request from Japanese Prime Minister Tomiichi Murayama to apologize for dropping the bomb, but his administration, responding to complaints from Japan, directed the Postal Service to cancel a commemorative mushroom-cloud postage stamp. The official language of anniversary ceremonies will drop the traditional "V-J Day" [Victory over Japan] in favor of "End of the Pacific War." At the same time, however, the design of an exhibit at the Smithsonian [National Air and Space Museum in Washington, D.C.], centered on the B-29 bomber that dropped the atomic bomb on Hiroshima, was curtailed after veterans' groups protested the inclusion of "revisionist" material that would have described the United States as waging a war of vengeance.

> It may be that there will never be a consensus about either the facts of the case or the morality of the decision.

It is because of the enormous consequences of the decision to use the bomb in the way it was used that controversy has continued for five decades; it may be that there will never be a consensus about either the facts of the case or the morality of the decision. . . .

For some, the issues of historical fact raised by these questions are central to the making of a moral judgment on the use of the atomic bomb, or, rather the use of both bombs. If it can be shown that using the bomb shortened the war, averting the need for a land invasion and the loss of many thousands of lives on both sides, the moral issue is settled.

For others, to be sure, that is not a sufficient moral criterion. For them any deliberate attack on noncombatants is wrong regardless of consequences, including the possibility that dropping the bomb saved lives, even civilian lives, overall. . . .

The Decision to Use the Atomic Bomb

President Franklin D. Roosevelt [FDR] made the basic decision to use the bomb in October 1939, when he initiated the Manhattan Project to counter Germany's atomic program and, in FDR's words, "to see that the Nazis don't blow us up." Roosevelt planned to use the atomic bomb. Secretary Stimson recalled, "At no time from 1941–45 did I ever hear it suggested by the president, or any other responsible member of the government that atomic energy should not be used in war." If the atomic bomb had been ready it would have been dropped on Germany. . . .

The atomic age began on July 16, 1945, near Alamogordo, New Mexico. Minutes after witnessing the bomb test, General Thomas Farrell said to General [Leslie] Groves, "The war is over!" "Yes," replied Groves, "it is over as soon as we drop two bombs on Japan."

In Potsdam, Germany, where he was attending a summit conference with [British prime minister Winston] Churchill and [Soviet premier] Joseph Stalin, Truman, according to Stimson, "was tremendously pepped up" by news of the successful test. After he studied a full report of the New Mexico test, Truman met with his advisers to make final plans for the use of the bomb. Truman explained, "I called a meeting to discuss what should be done with this awful weapon. I asked General [George] Marshall what it would cost in lives to land on the Tokyo plain and other places in Japan. It was his opinion that such an invasion would cost, at a minimum, one quarter of a million casualties and might cost as much as a million on the American side alone with an equal number of the enemy. The other military and naval men present agreed."

General Dwight Eisenhower and Admiral William Leahy, chairman of the Joint Chiefs of Staff, opposed using the bomb. Eisenhower believed the A-bomb was unnecessary to defeat Japan and he joined Leahy in rejecting its use on moral grounds. But Truman gained Churchill's unequivocal support. Churchill explained "there was never a moment's discussion as to whether the atomic bomb should be used or not. The final decision now lay in the main with President Truman, who had the weapon, but I never doubted what it would be nor have I doubted that he was right." . . .

General Groves's role in the decision-making process is crucial. He originated the two-bomb plan, and he wrote the order directing that a second bomb (and succeeding bombs) be used as soon as possible after August 3. After Groves's directive was sent to the bomb team on

July 25, only a countermanding order from Marshall, Stimson, or Truman could halt the process. . . .

The Use of the Bomb Forced Japan's Surrender

On August 6, Hiroshima was destroyed. More than 100,000 Japanese and two American POW's were killed. . . .

Meanwhile, the bomb team hurried to obey the order to "use additional bombs as soon as made ready by the project staff." The second bomb was scheduled for August 20, but the date was moved to August 11 when the necessary fissionable material arrived. According to Groves, "It became apparent that we could probably slice another day from our schedule." A round-the-clock effort readied the second bomb on August 9, less than three days after Hiroshima. Time was the sole controlling factor in determining when the second bomb would be dropped. Groves stressed, "Admiral [William H.] Purnell [Blandy] and I had often discussed the importance of having the second blow follow the first one quickly so that the Japanese would not have time to recover their balance."

On August 9, Nagasaki was obliterated. More than 35,000 Japanese were killed immediately and approximately 25,000 have since died as a consequence of the bomb. Forty-four percent of Nagasaki was destroyed.

Was the atomic bomb necessary to compel Japan to surrender? Or were the merciless bombardment of the Japanese coast and the strangling blockade of Japan by the Pacific fleet the key factors? Or were the ferocious fire bomb raids on Japan's cities by fleets of B-29s the basic reason for surrender? Did Japan finally capitulate because the Soviet Union declared war against her on August 8?

All these factors were important in defeating Japan, but in my opinion a defeated Japan was forced to surren-

Emperor Hirohito

During World War II, Emperor Hirohito of Japan was despised and vilified by the American public as the symbol of Japanese treachery and atrocities, and was generally considered comparable to Adolf Hitler. But unlike Hitler, he was not a dictator, and historians disagree about the extent to which he was responsible for the conduct of the war. The official religion of Japan taught that the imperial family was descended from the sun goddess, so the emperor was viewed as divine; yet his role in the government was largely ceremonial. The real power was held by the Cabinet, which was dominated by hawkish military leaders.

Some historians believe that Hirohito agreed with the Cabinet and followed military tactics closely, while others say he never wanted to attack the United States and distanced himself as much from military concerns as he did from contact with his people. In any case, near the end of the war Hirohito wanted to seek peace, hoping the terms could be made more favorable to Japan through negotiation. When that failed, he broke with custom by overruling the Cabinet to insist on immediate surrender.

After the war, the United States did not try Hirohito as a war criminal and allowed him to remain the ceremonial head of state in democratized Japan, believing that this would unify the Japanese people. He was required only to deny his divine descent. In the following years, Hirohito became more active in public life and traveled abroad to meet foreign leaders. He devoted much of his time to his main interest, marine biology, and published a number of scientific papers. He remained emperor until his death in 1989 at the age of eighty-seven, having reigned for sixty-two years, and was succeeded by his son Akihito. In accordance with Japanese tradition, he was given a new name after his death and is now known as Emperor Shōwa.

der by the Hiroshima atomic bomb. Japan finally gave up because the Japanese emperor ordered surrender.

And it was the Hiroshima atomic bomb that spurred Emperor Hirohito to make this bold decision. Before Hiroshima, none of the horrors of war visited upon Japan prompted the emperor to act—not the defeat of the Japa-

nese army on Okinawa in June, the destruction of Japan's cities, the starvation blockade, or the threat of a massive allied invasion of the home islands. After Hiroshima, nothing else—neither the entry of the Soviet Union into the war against Japan on August 8 nor the Nagasaki bomb on August 9—was needed to convince Hirohito to order surrender.

Only Japan's Emperor Could Overrule the Military

A study of the frantic last days of World War II shows clearly the indispensable role played by the Hiroshima bomb and proves the irrelevance of the Nagasaki bomb. Japan's military situation in August 1945 was desperate. Her cities had been devastated by B-29 attacks. The air massacre of Tokyo on March 9 by 350 B-29s dropping tons of magnesium, phosphorus, and napalm bombs was the single most destructive air attack of the war. Over 100,000 Japanese perished in the fire storm where ground temperatures reached 2,000 degrees. By May, three more mass bombings of Tokyo leveled half of the city.

Japan's supply of weapons was nearly depleted by the summer of 1945, her oil reserves were drained, and the country was isolated by a tight naval blockade of the coast. Food was scarce; starvation was imminent. Japan's once proud navy rested on the Pacific floor, and her army had been beaten back to the home islands in an unbroken series of shattering defeats. More than 3 million Japanese had been killed, 1 million in the last eight months of the war.

But despite all this carnage and ruin, Japan clung to the Homeland Battle Strategy Plan, approved by the cabinet and sanctioned by the emperor in February 1945, to fight "a decisive battle in the homeland even at the cost of self-destruction of the entire Japanese race." In June, Japan's military leaders secured cabinet and imperial approval for "The Fundamental Policy to Be Followed

Photo on previous page: The city of Nagasaki was reduced to rubble by the atomic blast in August 1945. (Bettman/Corbis.)

Henceforth in the Conduct of the War" calling for "100 million people to arise from the vantage ground of their sacred land to strike the invaders dead."

Japan's civilian leaders favored surrender, but even after the fall of Okinawa and the demolition of Japan's cities by B-29 raids, they could not convince the powerful military chiefs. Keeper of the Privy Seal Koichi Kido knew "only the intervention by the emperor" could overrule the military leaders and end the war.

Because of this deadlock, surrender through normal channels was impossible. Decision-making power in wartime Japan rested exclusively with the fifteen-member cabinet, composed of military and civilian leaders, where unanimous consent was required. The Japanese emperor merely heard and automatically approved unanimous decisions already reached by the cabinet. According to Deputy Foreign Minister Toshikazu Kase, "The emperor was always a dummy who sat through the sessions without ever taking an active part."

But in August 1945, Emperor Hirohito, through his prestige as a high priest and "father of the Japanese people," decided the issue of peace or war. However, before Hirohito could be stimulated to end the war he needed to be shocked. The Hiroshima atomic bomb provided that shock.

The Atomic Bombing Caused the Emperor to Intervene

Truman's critics have argued that he could have negotiated an end to the war without using the atomic bombs if he had conditioned surrender by allowing Japan to preserve the imperial institution. . . .

While Japan's leaders were debating surrender terms, they learned that Nagasaki had been bombed. Still, [General Korechika] Anami, [General Yoshijiro] Umezu, and [Admiral Soemu] Toyoda would not give way. General Umezu argued that Japanese soldiers could not surrender, explaining that they were indoctrinated to believe that "if they lost their weapons they should fight with their feet; if they couldn't fight with these, they should bite, and if they could not, [they] should cut out their tongues and kill themselves." . . .

The night of August 9, by prearranged plan, Prime Minister Suzuki convened an imperial conference, even though the cabinet was unable to report a decision to the emperor on surrender. . . . After three hours of impassioned but inconclusive debate, Prime Minister Suzuki asked the emperor to resolve the issue of surrender. Hirohito's words startled the military leaders: "I cannot bear to see my innocent people suffer any longer. I swallow my own tears and give sanction to the proposal to accept the Allied proclamation on the basis outlined by the foreign minister."

The emperor's godlike status and his spiritual influence with the people was overwhelming; Emperor Hirohito's will could not be denied. Therefore, the cabinet approved the emperor's decision to surrender. Suzuki informed the United States on August 10 of the cabinet's acceptance of the Potsdam Proclamation "with the understanding that the said declaration does not compromise any demand which prejudices the prerogatives of his majesty as supreme ruler." . . .

In his answer to Japan's surrender proposal, Truman hedged on the status of the emperor, ordering that "from the moment of surrender the authority of the emperor and the Japanese government to rule the state shall be subject to the supreme commander of the Allied powers who will take such steps as he deems proper to effectuate surrender terms."

> "Without the emperor's intervention, Japan would not have surrendered, and without the Hiroshima bomb, the emperor would not have intervened."

Even Japan's moderates opposed Truman's provision that the emperor "shall be subject to the supreme commander of the Allied powers." Japan's leaders again disagreed over conditions for surrender. Fanatical officers clamored for a fight to the finish with the United States. Admiral Takijiro Onishi, vice-chief of the Naval General Staff, pleaded with Foreign Minister Togo to "let us formulate a plan for certain victory, obtain the emperor's sanction, and throw ourselves into bringing the plan to realization. If we are prepared to sacrifice 20 million Japanese lives in a special attack effort, victory shall be ours."

After the cabinet was again unable to reach a decision on surrender, a second Imperial Conference was held on August 14. This time the emperor's decision finally ended World War II. Hirohito explained sorrowfully, "I cannot endure the thought of letting my people suffer any longer. A continuation of the war would bring death to tens, perhaps even hundreds of thousands of persons. The whole nation would be reduced to ashes."

Twenty years after the war, Kido, the emperor's close adviser, explained, "the presence of the atomic bomb made it easier for us politicians to negotiate peace. Even then the military would not listen to reason. The only reason the Japanese Army stopped fighting was because the emperor ordered them to do so." Without the emperor's intervention, Japan would not have surrendered, and without the Hiroshima bomb, the emperor would not have intervened.

The Nagasaki Bomb Had No Role in the Surrender

If the Hiroshima bomb caused the emperor to order Japan to surrender, what role did the Nagasaki bomb play? None. The Nagasaki bomb had no influence on Emperor Hirohito's determination after Hiroshima to end the war, nor did it convince Japan's military leaders, who opposed surrender to the end. The Nagasaki bomb was irrelevant in ending World War II. Obviously, Truman did not know the details of Japan's internal struggle to surrender in August 1945, but based on information available to American leaders at the time the second bomb was dropped, no moral, military, or diplomatic standard justified its use. . . .

Truman allowed Japan no time to surrender between atomic bombs; the Nagasaki bomb was used as soon as it was ready. Truman's order of July 25 commanded the bomb crew to use "additional bombs as soon as they are made available by the project staff." Had the second bomb been ready on August 7, it would have been dropped then, for General Groves admitted he wanted the second bomb to "follow the first one quickly so that the Japanese would not have time to recover their balance." . . .

Groves's second argument for using the Nagasaki bomb was, "one bomb would be necessary to show the Japanese the power of the bomb, and the second would be needed to show them that we had the capacity to make more than one. In other words, that it is not a single laboratory achievement." But if the Nagasaki weapon was used to prove to Japan that the United States had an atomic arsenal, the second bomb could have been dropped on an uninhabited area, not on a densely populated city.

Groves's third reason for bombing Nagasaki was: "It was not at all obvious prior to this time [before the Nagasaki bomb] that the war was over. We had little information as to the damage the first bomb had inflicted in Hiroshima."

Perhaps Groves was unaware before August 9 of the full damage at Hiroshima, but Truman knew the extent of the destruction and had time to stop the Nagasaki attack. On August 6, Truman had been notified while returning by ship from Potsdam that Hiroshima had been bombed successfully. Said Secretary of State [James] Byrnes, "His report indicated that the results of the bomb were even more successful than the test had led us to expect." On August 8, Truman studied more information about the destruction of Hiroshima, including Air Force photographs that revealed clearly the vast area of devastation.

The Nagasaki story shows that America's leaders, understandably obsessed with ending the war quickly, failed to use the second atomic bomb rationally or tactically. No high-level discussion was held to consider the second bomb. Nobody challenged or reviewed the informal, unofficial, and premature judgment of General Groves, reached in December 1944, to drop two atomic bombs. . . .

After Hiroshima, their fingers were frozen on the atomic trigger despite rational arguments that shouted for delay and reconsideration.

The Use of Only One Bomb Was Necessary

The United States has been wrongly condemned for needlessly introducing atomic war. Without the Hiroshima bomb to spur the emperor to demand surrender, an allied land invasion of Japan would have been launched. The invasion plan had been completed by the Joint Chiefs of Staff in May 1945, and approved by President Truman on June 18. . . . Had an invasion of Japan occurred, the carnage on both sides would have been catastrophic. Japan was prepared for a kamikaze defense of the home islands. In August, Japan had 2.5 million troops on the main islands backed by 9,000 kamikaze planes and a 32-million civilian militia sworn to fight for the emperor with spears, muskets, bows and arrows, and even so-called "Sherman carpets," children with dynamite strapped to their bodies and trained to throw themselves under American tanks. . . .

The number of American troops killed in an invasion of Japan would certainly have doubled the 50,000 who died in combat in the entire Pacific war.

The potential civilian losses are even more grim. On Okinawa, approximately 140,000 of the island's 450,000 residents (31 percent) were killed as the American and Japanese armies ravaged the island. For the homeland battle, millions of Japanese civilians were trained and determined to "strike the invaders dead." Using the "Okinawa formula," approximately 27.9 million of Japan's 90 million people might have died in the final battle.

Whether 40,000 or 500,000 American troops would have been killed in an invasion of Japan, for moral and political reasons the president could not allow American fighting men to die in battle while he withheld the atomic bomb, a weapon he believed would end the war. Truman explained, "The use of the atomic bomb was a military decision to end the war and save millions of lives. It was just the same as getting a bigger gun than the other fellow had to win the war and that's what it was used for. I never lost any sleep over my decision." . . .

> America's stature today would be higher, and 60,000 lives would have been saved at Nagasaki, had President Truman waited for the Hiroshima bomb to work its effect on Japan's leaders.

In my view, which is one based ultimately on the overall loss of life and not on the principle of noncombatant immunity, the United States was justified in using the atomic bomb. The Hiroshima bomb shocked Emperor Hirohito into breaking the political impasse in the Japanese cabinet and ordering surrender. The Hiroshima bomb ended World War II in the Pacific, and thus, prevented a ferocious land battle on mainland Japan. But America's stature today would be higher, and 60,000 lives would have been saved at Nagasaki, had President Truman waited for the Hiroshima bomb to work its effect on Japan's leaders.

When General Eisenhower expressed his strong opposition to dropping the bomb on Japan, telling Secretary Stimson, "It wasn't necessary to hit them with that awful thing," he was wrong. It was—once, but not twice.

Majority Opinion Across the Political Spectrum Initially Favored Use of the Atomic Bomb

Paul F. Boller, Jr.

> In the following excerpt from his book on myths of American history, Paul Boller points out that, contrary to common belief, the atomic bombing of Hiroshima was originally applauded by the political left as well as the right. He quotes from Communist and liberal publications to illustrate how widely the political left approved of the bombings until twenty years later, when it was reconsidered in the light of opposition to the Vietnam War. Though some liberals deplored the bombings from the beginning, they were only a small minority. Boller is a professor emeritus of history at Texas Christian University and the author of many popular books on US history. While in the navy during World War II, he served as a Japanese translator.

SOURCE. Paul F. Boller, Jr., "Hiroshima and the American Left," *Not So! Popular Myths About America from Columbus to Clinton*. Oxford University Press, 1995, pp. 147–153. Reproduced by permission.

In August 1945, American rightists applauded and American leftists denounced President [Harry S.] Truman's decision to authorize the dropping of atomic bombs on Japan.

Not so.

The majority of Americans, on both the left and the right, approved of Truman's action at the time, as a way of ending the war with Japan quickly. Some conservatives—former President Herbert Hoover and *U.S. News* editor David Lawrence—deplored the action, and some liberals—popular economist Stuart Chase and *Christian Science Monitor* correspondent Richard L. Strout—did so too. But most Americans felt as *Time, Newsweek*, the *New York Times*, and other mainstream publications did: the bombs dropped on Hiroshima and Nagasaki were horrible weapons, but they did end the war promptly, obviated the necessity of invading Japan, and thus saved countless lives, Japanese as well as American. . . .

> The majority of Americans, on both the left and the right, approved of Truman's action at the time, as a way of ending the war with Japan quickly.

Opinion Against the Atomic Bombings Arose in the 1960s

Twenty years after Hiroshima, Americans on the left began having second thoughts about the atomic bombs. In New Leftist circles in the late 1960s, protests against U.S. involvement in Vietnam began to spill over into criticism of U.S. policies during World War II and finally came to focus on Hiroshima. In a book entitled *Atomic Diplomacy: Hiroshima and Potsdam*, published in 1965, historian Gar Alperowitz presented the thesis that Japan was thoroughly beaten by August 1945 and the use of atomic bombs was unnecessary for ending the war, and that the main reason the United States dropped the bombs was to intimidate the USSR. "Atomic diplomacy," in short, not military necessity, dictated Truman's action. Alperowitz's "revisionist" views about the atom bombs quickly took root among New Leftists and soon became conventional wisdom for many leftists in this country and abroad. "The bombing of Hiroshima," wrote political philosopher Michael Walzer, in a typical view, in 1989, "was an act of terrorism; its purpose was political, not military." By then, men and women of goodwill were in the habit of gathering in towns and cities throughout the country on August 6—Hiroshima Day—in atonement for the dropping of atomic bombs on Japan and to renew their dedication to the cause of world peace.

The charge that the United States made use of atomic bombs when it didn't need to is of course a horrendous one. It places the United States, for cold and calculated brutality, in the same category as Nazi Germany and militaristic Japan. But the charge is also a breathtakingly *ex post facto* [after the fact] one. It certainly wasn't made by American leftists (the spiritual ancestors of the New Leftists) in August 1945. No one on the left, including American Stalinists, dreamed of talking about "atomic diplomacy" against the Soviet Union in 1945. Ironically, in fact, those liberals and radicals who were friendliest to Stalinist Russia in 1945 were also the most enthusiastic about the use of atomic bombs on Japan, while those who were the most critical of the Stalinist system were also the most sharply critical of the United States for dropping the bombs on Japan.

Leftist Publications Approved of the Bombing in 1945

Take, for example, the *Daily Worker*. Official organ of the American Communist Party (CP, USA), and unswervingly loyal to the policies and principles laid down by Soviet dictator Josef Stalin, the *Worker* had none of the misgivings that Herbert Hoover did about the use of atomic bombs on Hiroshima and Nagasaki. Wrote the

paper's military analyst right after the Hiroshima strike: "We are lucky we have found the Thing and are able to speed the war against the Japanese before the enemy can devise countermeasures. Thank God for that." And he added: "So let us not greet our atomic device with a shudder, but with the elation and admiration which the genius of man deserves." The *New Masses*, the Communist Party's biweekly, published in New York, was equally gleeful about the atomic bomb. The bomb, said the editors, was a "symbol of the great potentialities that can be

A rejection of the atomic bombings of Japan was among the positions embraced by the protest movements of the 1960s. (**Associated Press.**)

released once the energies of the people are fully tapped." For both the *Daily Worker* and the *New Masses*, however, the dropping of atomic bombs on Hiroshima and Nagasaki was dwarfed by the entry of the Soviet Union into the war about the time of Nagasaki. From then on they took the line that Russia's last-minute intervention in the war, not the atomic bombs, played the crucial role in forcing Japan's capitulation.

The joy which the *Daily Worker* and the *New Masses* experienced on the news of Japan's abrupt capitulation on August 14 was marred, however, by President Truman's decision to compromise with Japan at the last moment in order to hasten the surrender. Instead of hewing to the "unconditional surrender" policy proclaimed by President Roosevelt in 1943 (and warmly supported by CP, USA), the Truman administration decided to let the Japanese retain their emperor after the war instead of trying him as a war criminal.

> For [leftist publications in 1945] it was the atomic bombs that produced sudden victory and they saw no need to apologize for their use.

The American Communists bitterly criticized the Truman administration for scuttling the unconditional-surrender policy and letting the emperor off so easily. . . .

The most influential non-Communist leftist publications in 1945 were the *Nation* and the *New Republic*, liberal weeklies, and *PM*, Manhattan's liberal daily. Though following no line but their own, all three publications were extremely sympathetic to the Soviet Union and anxious to promote good relations between the United States and the Soviets during and after the war. Not only did they regard the Soviet Union as on the whole a progressive and peace-loving society; they also reminded their readers that the USSR had lost millions of people beating back the Nazi invaders during the European war. Like the Stalinist *Daily Worker* and the *New Masses*, the pro-Soviet (but non-Stalinist) *Nation, New Republic,* and *PM* warmly greeted the use of atomic bombs on Japan, and they also tended to see eye to eye with the Stalinists on unconditional surrender and the sacking of the Japanese emperor. They disagreed, however, with the Stalinists in thinking Russia's last-minute intervention played a crucial part in bringing about Japan's decision to surrender. For them, it was the atomic bombs that produced sudden victory and they saw no need to apologize for their use.

To say that the *Nation,* the *New Republic,* and *PM* approved of the bombing of Hiroshima and Nagasaki is to understate the matter. All three publications took for granted from the outset the necessity and desirability of the bombings. Only when some Americans expressed misgivings about the bombs did they move on to a positive defense of the bombings. "The bomb that hurried Russia into the Far Eastern war and drove Japan to surrender," wrote Freda Kirchwey, editor of the *Nation,* "has accomplished the specific job for which it was created. From the point of view of military strategy, $2,000,000,000 (the cost of the bomb and the cost of nine days of war) was never better spent. The suffering, the wholesale slaughter it entailed, have been outweighed by its spectacular success. Allied leaders can rightly claim that the loss of life on both sides would have been many times greater if the atomic bomb had not been used and Japan had gone on fighting. There is no answer to this argument."

The *New Republic* agreed with the *Nation.* Not only did the editors insist that the bombs saved countless lives by shortening the war; they also scoffed at charges by the Japanese that the bombs dropped on Hiroshima and Nagasaki had impregnated the soil with radioactivity which would be harmful to life for years to come. Pointing out that American scientists denied the allegation, the editors sarcastically proposed a way of settling the matter.

The First Widely-Read Stories of Hiroshima Survivors

A year after World War II ended, a leading American weekly magazine published a striking description of what life was like for those who survived a nuclear attack. The article, simply titled "Hiroshima," was published by *The New Yorker* in its August 31, 1946, issue. The thirty-one thousand word article displaced virtually all other editorial matter in the issue. "Hiroshima" traced the experiences of six residents who survived the blast . . . starting from when the six woke up that morning, to what they were doing the moment of the blast and the next few hours, continuing through the next several days and then ending with the situations of the six survivors several months later.

The article, written by John Hersey, created a blast of its own in the publishing world. *The New Yorker* sold out immediately, and requests for reprints poured in from all over the world. Following publication, "Hiroshima" was read on the radio in the United States and abroad. Other magazines reviewed the article and referred their readers to it. The Book-of-the-Month Club sent a copy of the article in book form to its entire membership as a free selection. Later that fall, "Hiroshima" was published as a book by Alfred A. Knopf and has remained in print ever since. . . .

The direct effect of "Hiroshima" on the American public is difficult to gauge. No mass movement formed as a result of the article . . . but certainly the vivid depictions in the book must have been a strong contributor to a pervasive sense of dread (and guilt) about nuclear weaponry felt by many Americans ever since August 1945.

SOURCE. *Steve Rothman, "The Publication of 'Hiroshima' in* The New Yorker," *herseyhiroshima.com, January 8, 1997.*

"If radioactivity is present in the soil," they wrote, "such plants will be marked by an unusual number of spots and mutations. Here is the ideal job for Emperor Hirohito, an amateur geneticist, after we are through with him— which, one hopes, will be soon. Let him go to Hiroshima, sit among the ruins, and watch the mutations grow."

The editorial writers and columnists for the feisty, pro-Soviet *PM* saw things much as the liberal weeklies did. "Thank God, It's Our Atomic Bomb!" exclaimed Irving Brant in an essay by that title for *PM* right after the Hiroshima strike. "Our atomic bomb! Do we realize, can we realize, what that little possessive pronoun means? Three little letters, o-u-r, to reflect the thankfulness of all Americans and of their allies that Germany or Japan did not produce this engine of inconceivable destruction." As to the regrets by some Americans about the use of atomic bombs on Japan, *PM*'s editors pointed out that the head of Japan's leading news agency had announced that the effect of the bombs was not as "good—bad—as is claimed," and that the B-29 raids on Tokyo on March 10 had done far more damage. "The few people who thought up, made, and dropped the atomic bomb," declared Max Lerner, in the first of two lead editorials for *PM* on the subject, "did more to bring Japan to its knees than the American fleet and (despite [Russian newspaper] *Isvestiya*'s recent denial) the massive Russian armies." In his second piece on the subject, Lerner conceded the horror of the atomic bombs as weapons of war, but insisted that their use was justified because "we used the atom bomb," not out of "hatred and sadism," but "to end the war quickly, and with a loathing for its needs."

Some Liberals Deplored the Atomic Bombings

Not all American liberals agreed with Lerner. America's religious liberals, for one, felt sorrow, not elation, over the atomic bombings and thought they had destroyed the nation's moral position in the world: *Commonweal*, a Catholic weekly with a liberal social outlook, and the *Christian Century*, a liberal Protestant weekly published in Chicago. There were secular liberals, too, writing for weekly magazines with a small circulation—*Common Sense*, published in New York, and the *Progressive*, published in Madison, Wisconsin—who also deplored the atomic bombings. The anti-Hiroshima liberals, religious and secular, criticized both the United States and the Soviet Union for ignoring Japanese peace bids earlier in the year, and they also thought the United States should have arranged a demonstration of the effectiveness of the atomic bomb in order to persuade Japan to surrender before Hiroshima. Socialist leader Norman Thomas (a staunch anti-Stalinist) shared their views. "I shall be told that it was the bomb which ended the war," he declared. "As things were that is probably true, but I shall always believe that the war might have been ended before the first atomic bomb was dropped on Hiroshima bringing death to at least a hundred thousand men, women, and children."

The United States Owes Japan No Apology for Using the Atomic Bomb

Neil Steinberg

In the following viewpoint, newspaper columnist Neil Steinberg comments on the heated controversy over the exhibit of the *Enola Gay* at the Smithsonian Institution's Air and Space Museum. The controversy continued over a number of years, resulting in many revisions to the exhibit's content. Veterans and others objected to the original exhibit on grounds that it focused on the Japanese casualties at Hiroshima rather than on the reasons for the atomic bombing and its role in ending World War II. The version of the exhibit discussed by Steinberg drew objections for the opposite reason. The United States criticizes its past actions too much, he says. In his opinion, Japan brought atomic bombing on itself by its previous atrocities, and US actions should be put in perspective. Steinberg is a columnist for the *Chicago Sun-Times* and the author of several books.

SOURCE. Neil Steinberg, "U.S. Owes Japan No Apology at Hiroshima Plane Exhibit," *Jewish World Review*, 2003. Reproduced by permission.

There is a museum in Tokyo dedicated to Japan's ample history of warfare. But if you visit the plainly named Military Museum, you will find no reference to the grotesque medical experiments the Japanese army conducted in World War II or the sex slaves it kidnapped. The Rape of Nanking, when rampaging Japanese troops raped and murdered hundreds of thousands of Chinese, is airbrushed into the "Nanking Incident" and the facts are said to be uncertain. Civilian deaths aren't mentioned at all until the Americans begin firebombing Tokyo in 1944.

This is par for the course. In Japanese textbooks the relentless quest of military domination that so marked that nation's conduct in the 20th century gently morphs into a brave struggle for independence against a hostile world.

Nor is the museum a relic of the equivocating past. It opened just last year. "The museum's jingoism [extreme nationalism] begins in the very first room," wrote Howard French in the *New York Times*. "There, a saber adorned with gold braid, an ancient relic from the Imperial Palace guard, hangs, dramatically lit, above a block of text glorifying 2,600 years of independence, secured by valiant warriors against unnamed invaders."

So it is irony of the most extreme sort that Japanese survivors of the atomic bomb are unhappy with how the Smithsonian Institution [in Washington, D.C.] is displaying the Enola Gay, the B-29 Superfortress that dropped the first atomic bomb used in war on Hiroshima, in its new Air and Space Museum annex next to Dulles Airport.

They would like photos of radiation burns and stats of the 160,000 who died in the first atomic blast next to the airplane.

"As victims of the A-bombs, we can't bear to have the Enola Gay, which killed thousands of Hiroshima residents, on public display without including details of the

destruction it wrought," said Terumi Tnaka, the Japan Confederation of A-Bomb and H-Bomb Sufferers Organization's director.

The Smithsonian's display of the *Enola Gay*, which dropped the Hiroshima bomb, ignited intense controversy. (**Associated Press.**)

This is not an obscure issue of museum policy. History is an argument—a war, so to speak. The battles of the past continue in the present in symbolic form, as academics, survivors, and regular people struggle to decide how a thing will be remembered.

It is a war, I'm sad to say, that America is losing. Most nations make their history into a flattering story they tell themselves. Japan isn't even the most extreme case—history in North Korea is a fairy tale honoring a madman. And we all know what kids learned in school in Iraq up until last spring [2003, i.e., prior to the War in Iraq].

Americans Like to Beat Themselves Up

The United States, however, is different, possibly unique, with the arguable exception of Germany, in how we view our past. Because of our standards and sensitivities, we paint a picture of ourselves that is extraordinarily bleak. Not only have the Japanese complained, but some American academics argued that the Enola Gay should not be displayed without slapping ourselves around.

This fits perfectly with the standard public school version of America: a nightmare of slavery and broken treaties, relieved only by the unsung bravery of pioneer girls and Indian fighters, who are the true heroes of our history, as opposed to dead white males such as slave-owner George Washington and whoremonger Thomas Jefferson.

Such a skewed dismissal is as bad as Japanese self-glory. History should not be a whitewash, but it shouldn't be self-flagellation either. The United States has made mistakes, but those missteps need to be put into the greater story of the miracle that is our country. We need a balance—otherwise our children grow up needlessly abashed, just as Japanese children grow up with a view of their country that enormously diverges from both fact and the perception of the rest of the world.

> The United States does indeed have things to be ashamed of. But World War II is not one of them.

It's Called the "Good War" for a Reason

The United States does indeed have things to be ashamed of. But World War II is not one of them. Shameful chapters—such as the internment of our own Japanese citizens—must be compared to the unchecked brutality in much of the world at the time. Before we honor the victimhood of others, we should honor our own. Before some group of A-bomb survivors guilts the Smithsonian into kneeling on a rail over the atomic bomb, I wish a delegation of Bataan Death March survivors or men maimed at Pearl Harbor would whisper their side.

Perhaps the Enola Gay should be displayed next to that photo of a Chinese baby wailing in the rubble of a Japanese bombing, as a reminder of how the Japanese had very methodically removed themselves from the pale of humanity over a period of years before the bomb dropped. Perhaps the Enola Gay should be shown next to photos of kamikaze planes and descriptions of how surrendering Japanese would pull the pins on grenades, or next to tales of Iwo Jima and Saipan and all the miserable chunks of rock that U.S. Marines died trying to pry away from the Japanese death grip. Harry Truman, a haberdasher from Missouri, perhaps the most ordinary American ever to serve in the presidency, was absolutely right to drop the bomb. The Japanese nation earned the Enola Gay's visit. The rest is just present day politics and the posturing of those not in any position to complain.

CHAPTER 3

Personal Narratives

Working to Develop the Atomic Bomb

Paul Olum

In the following viewpoint, Paul Olum, a researcher who participated in the development of the atomic bomb, tells what it was
like at the Los Alamos Laboratory, where some of the greatest
scientists of the time were working. He also talks about why
they were willing to continue the project even after they knew
the bomb would not be needed to defeat German dictator Adolf
Hitler. Although the justification for the development of the
bomb no longer existed, he says, the scientists were unwilling to
stop a project they had almost finished. Olum was a mathema-
tician and university administrator. For some years before his
retirement, he was president of the University of Oregon.

Photo on previous
page: When he died
in 2010, Tsutomu
Yamaguchi was the
only person officially
recognized as having
survived the bombings
of both Hiroshima and
Nagasaki. (**Associated
Press.**)

T he Los Alamos Scientific Laboratory opened in
April, 1943. Its charge was straightforward, but
quite unlike anything before in history: to do the
basic scientific and technical research necessary to deter-

SOURCE. Paul Olum, "Hiroshima: Memoir of a Bomb Maker . . . The
Gadget," *History News Network*, 2001. Reproduced by permission.

mine whether a nuclear bomb could be constructed; and, if that appeared feasible, to build such bombs when the material for them became available. I joined the project as part of the theoretical physics group roughly a month before actual opening of the laboratory. . . .

I was young, 24, and still a graduate student at Princeton University in theoretical physics and mathematics. A very large share of the people there were quite young, in their 20s, even senior group leaders on the project like Richard Feynman and Robert Wilson; and many of the others were people in their 30s. Robert Oppenheimer, the Director, was relatively old for the group, in his late 30s.

An Extraordinary Scientific Community

Los Alamos was an extraordinary place. It is in an isolated area of New Mexico, some distance north of Santa Fe, up on a mesa. The whole area was fenced in, and there were military guards and strict security at the gates. There was no way to get in or out without passing through these security checks.

We weren't even allowed to tell our parents and friends where we were going. All we could say was that we were somewhere in the continental United States, the actual location a secret. Our parents wrote to us by writing to Princeton; one person collected the mail there and forwarded it to an appropriate place in Santa Fe from which the mail was gotten to us. Later, they could write to Santa Fe. All mail, incoming and outgoing, was censored, the only place within the United States where such censorship took place.

The strict security had an important scientific purpose, namely that by restricting totally, at least in principle, all communication with the outside world, it was possible to have a completely free flow of information among the scientific staff inside the laboratory. Oppenheimer insisted on that, and it was important evidence of the strength of his leadership that he could pull it off, because the military and, in particular, Gen. [Leslie] Groves, head of the Manhattan Project, could hardly stand the notion that everyone on the scientific staff could talk to everyone else, and discuss what they were doing. This was not the Army's way of running a secret project. However, it was extraordinarily important that we were able to do so because out of such interchanges and out of all our open seminars and conferences came the creative new ideas which made success ultimately possible. The result is that all of us knew just what was going on and what we all were doing. From the beginning, we knew we were building a bomb which could destroy a whole city, could kill hundreds of thousands of people. We also knew that what we were building was unquestionably the most elementary, pre-model-T version of such a bomb, and that others more powerful surely would follow. We sat in meetings discussing how to maximize the deadly destructive power of this weapon. We knew then, when we stopped to think about it, what a terrible thing we were engaged in.

> We never called it a bomb, lest somehow the word should slip out in some unauthorized place. It was always referred to as 'the gadget.'

At the same time, all of these young people found themselves in the most unbelievable, most extraordinary scientific community ever collected in the world, except perhaps for brief international conferences lasting a few days. Some of the greatest names in physics were there. . . . To be in the company of these people, many of the world's greatest minds, was an incredible experience one never could have found anywhere else. . . .

Developing the Bomb

Many . . . problems had to be solved before it was possible to know whether or not [an atomic] bomb could be built. Incidentally, we never called it a bomb, lest somehow the word should slip out in some unauthorized place. It was always referred to as "the gadget." A crucial part of our problem was that there was no way to test this gadget in advance, or to test the functioning of parts of it. We had to do all of our experimental and theoretical planning on the basis of information at the atomic level, and could not know whether it would really work until it was all done and built. . . .

All of the time we were doing these things at Los Alamos, the fissionable material was being produced a tiny bit at a time at the huge plants at Oakridge and Hanford. At Oakridge, they were separating the Uranium 235 needed for a uranium bomb. At Hanford, they were creating from large nuclear piles the new Element 94, plutonium, which also underwent fission. Finally, by the middle of 1945, the fissionable material became available. In the meantime at Los Alamos, the research was being completed and plans made. The critical size was determined, and the difficult process of assembling a bomb was resolved. Assembly could be done one of two ways, either by putting one half in the mouth of a cannon and shooting the other half of it, or else by surrounding a sphere of loosely packed material with TNT and "imploding" it (i.e., compressing it very greatly at enormous speed). The latter was more tricky, but it was the only way that would work for plutonium.

Then, on July 16, 1945, at Alamogordo, New Mexico, the bomb test (code named "Trinity") was conducted. It was a plutonium bomb, because the project leaders were so worried about that one that they had to test it to be absolutely sure of it. I saw the test from many miles away, sitting on the side of a hill. The explosion was an incredible thing, and seemed at first to fill the whole of the sky,

> We knew if [the Germans] got it and could deliver it in their huge intercontinental rockets, they could very likely win the war, ultimately taking over the whole world.

so that those of us theoretical types who were watching from a distance (being of no use at the actual test) were momentarily afraid that all of our colleagues had been consumed by the blast.

Twenty-one days later, on Aug. 6, 1945, a bomb was dropped on Hiroshima, this time a uranium bomb. Three days later, on Aug. 9, a plutonium bomb was dropped on Nagasaki.

Why We Did It

That is a brief history of what happened. Why did we do it, why did we work to produce such a terrible weapon? Most of us were young, decent, moral people who surely did not want to kill anybody. We did not know exactly how many would die, but the fact perhaps 130,000 people died in the Hiroshima explosion was no surprise; that was the right order of magnitude with a bomb going off equivalent to 16–18,000 tons of TNT, maybe a little less. The Nagasaki bomb was somewhat more powerful, but killed fewer people, partly because of [the] geometry of the city.

Why did we let ourselves do such an incredibly awful thing, sitting there in our offices and conference rooms and talking about it, then doing experiments and calculations, moving step-by-step to the creation of this horror? Would I do it again if I had to? Do I feel now that it was a wrong thing to do?

I feel still today that there was no choice. We knew the Germans were working on a nuclear bomb, and that they had started as much as two years earlier than we. We knew it was possible they could get it. We knew if they got it and could deliver it in their huge intercontinental rockets, they could very likely win the war, ultimately taking over the whole world. I felt then there was indeed no choice, knowing that the Germans were doing it, and what [the] consequences would be for all of us if they got a nuclear bomb and we did not.

But that raises another question. When V.E. Day, victory in Europe, came in the spring of 1945, we were quite certain the Japanese had no bomb. The Japanese had hardly gotten anywhere toward building a bomb, and there was no belief they possibly could have one. Why didn't we all stop and walk off the project then? We no longer needed what we had been trying so hard to achieve. We didn't have to worry about somebody else getting it first. Nonetheless, I know of no one, none of the scientists at Los Alamos, none of our friends, who had to make such a decision. I suppose there are many reasons for what it was. Probably the best, and it is not one to be particularly proud of, is that when you are involved in something like that and carry it close to final creation, it just is hard to stop. You are totally caught up in it. You are making a bomb for a military purpose, for a war you are engaged in, and the war still is going on, and you haven't quite finished the job. I think very few of us stopped to think on V.E. Day that the justification we would have given for working on the bomb in the first place was no longer there. One might argue that if it wasn't built then, it would be built later. By April of 1945, it was essentially done, so why not see it through?

But I do think that in the main, it was actually the situation of scientists in the middle of an extraordinary project, unique in the world's history, wanting to see the results of what they had done.

Training as a Member of the *Enola Gay*'s Crew

Theodore "Dutch" Van Kirk

In the following viewpoint, Theodore "Dutch" Van Kirk, the navigator of the plane that dropped the atomic bomb on Hiroshima, talks about the training of the crews that were preparing for such missions and the effect the secrecy of the project had on it. In addition, he argues that Hiroshima contained many important military targets, including the Japanese army headquarters, and that even apart from the prospect of having to invade Japan, the atomic bombings saved lives. Heavy conventional bombing continued until Japan surrendered, he says, and large numbers of Japanese civilians would have been killed if the war had lasted even a short time longer. Van Kirk was a major in the US Army Air Corps.

There are a lot of myths that have grown up about the *Enola Gay* and about the dropping of the atomic bomb. I am going to puncture a few of

SOURCE. Theodore "Dutch" Van Kirk, "Hiroshima and the Enola Gay," *World War II Chronicles*, Winter 2005–2006. Reproduced by permission of the American Veterans Center.

The crew of the US Army B-29 *Enola Gay*, the bomber that dropped the atom bomb over Hiroshima, Japan. Captain Theodore Van Kirk stands second from left in the rear row. (**Associated Press.**)

them right now. One of them is that everything was about the *Enola Gay*, and only the *Enola Gay*. The *Enola Gay* was not the only thing we had in our arsenal. We had 15 bombing crews organized and trained to drop atomic weapons. In all, the 509th Composite Group had about 1,800 people total, all working to prepare for the deployment of the atomic bomb. We couldn't send our planes out to any other place to get operated on, so we needed crews who could perform maintenance to be stationed with us. This was primarily because of the secrecy of the project. If you looked at our airplanes, you knew that we were going to be doing something different. You look at the bomb bays, and there is only one hook up there. These planes were not going to go out and drop huge numbers of bombs along with the rest of the 20th Air Force. They had one purpose, for one mission.

Now, on to our training. When we arrived at our training site in Wendover, Utah, we were called together to meet with some of the scientists working on the project. One of the scientists said to us, "We think the airplane will be ok if you are eight miles away when the bomb explodes. We think." I remember looking at the guy and asking if he could be a little more definite than that! He replied that he didn't know. Some scientists believed that the bomb would start a chain reaction that would blow up the whole universe while some claimed that the bomb wouldn't do anything at all. We were not sure what to expect. That was our starting point.

Stripped-down Planes

To carry the bomb, we used stripped-down and modified B-29s. All of the extra weight that could possibly be removed was taken from the plane. Special engines were added, along with modified bomb bay doors. These were the best airplanes around at the time. Today, you can cruise around the world at 40,000 feet and think nothing of it. But back then, it wasn't so easy. The stripped-down planes were necessary to achieve the altitude and speed that would be needed to get away from the exploding bomb. There was absolutely no concern about the Japanese defenses at that time, so extra weaponry and defenses were useless. The key was to get away from the bomb as quickly as possible.

That brings up the second point. Keep in mind (and I am going to address my remarks to the young people in attendance), that the Japanese were a defeated nation long before we ever dropped the atomic bomb. If anybody ever tells you that the atomic bomb won World War

> What made this training special was that it was all about practicing the turn you needed to make in order to get away from the bomb.

II, you can tell them that they are full of malarkey. It did not. Eighty-five percent of the Japanese industrial capacity was burned down before we ever dropped the atomic bomb. Any reasonable people would have given up and accepted the terms of unconditional surrender before we ever dropped the atomic bomb. The Japanese government and military of that day were not reasonable in any sense of the word. It took the two atomic weapons and the deaths of about 200,000 people to convince them that they really were a defeated nation, and that they should accept the terms of unconditional surrender.

Back to the training. What made this training special was that it was all about practicing the turn you needed to make in order to get away from the bomb. In most bombing missions, you flew over your target, dropped the bombs, then continued on in a straight line. Had we done that with the atomic bomb, I would not be here today; it would have blown up the airplane. In this mission, we had to turn; we had to get away from it, and run as fast as we could. Even in that case, we felt two distinct shock waves from the blast.

Another major difference in our training was the issue of security. For example, every telephone line into and out of Wendover was tapped. You could not have a private conversation there if you wanted to. The secrecy of this mission was of such massive importance, that security was given top priority.

The Atomic Bombing Saved Lives

So why did we drop the atomic bomb? And why should we have dropped the atomic bomb? This is my opinion, and my opinion only. You will hear a lot of arguments about this from some history professors and teachers.

I value the opinions of many of them. However, many teachers just do not know what they are talking about, and have not taken the time to learn. I do not mind them expressing their personal opinions, but they should know all of the facts before making up their minds and expressing any opinion at all. It is understandable, with everything teachers need to do, that they cannot learn all the details about every single operation during World War II. However, I think that at least when speaking about something as important as the first atomic bomb, they should try to get that information correct.

Yes, 200,000 people were killed when the bombs were dropped. In Hiroshima, a lot of those people were part of the Japanese Army. We did not bomb Hiroshima simply to kill people. There were over 100 numbered military targets in the city of Hiroshima. The most important of these that we wanted to get was the Army headquarters. The Army was charged with the defense of Japan in case of invasion. And you know what that meant to our people if we had to invade—casualties unlike we had ever seen.

Now, even without the prospect of an American invasion of Japan, we still saved lives. It is not well known that the largest single air raid of the war over Japan was flown two days after the bombing of Nagasaki. Over 1,000 B-29s took part in the attack,

> Even if the war had only gone on another week, there would have been another seven [conventional] bombing raids that would have killed Japanese people.

including our modified planes. Since our planes were not equipped to handle regular bombs, we carried something called "pumpkins." They were the same size, weight, and shape as the atomic bomb, but were instead loaded with high explosives. There was so much air power over Japan at that time that not even a mouse would have been able to move without us bombing it. Think of the number of Japanese civilians that were killed on that raid that nobody ever heard about. I would almost bet money that as many people were killed on those raids than were killed at Hiroshima and Nagasaki. Raids like that would have continued every day the weather was clear until the war was over. I do not know when that would have been, but it certainly would not have been August 14 [1945]. Even if the war had only gone on another week, there would have been another seven bombing raids that would have killed Japanese people, no question about it. In addition to that, [General James] Doolittle was moving his 8th Air Force onto Okinawa, making all of Japan within range of his B-17s and B-24s. Japan had a decision to make. They could have starved to death, or they could be killed by atomic weapons. It was their choice.

Experiencing the Horrors of the Atomic Bombing

Keiko Murakami

In the following viewpoint, Keiko Murakami, who was eight years old when Hiroshima was bombed, tells what it was like when the bomb fell and how she and her family managed to survive. Her mother was badly injured, it was hard to get milk for her baby sister, and there was little if any food for the rest of the family. She and her brother walked miles out of the city to her grandfather's farm, finding it difficult to get through the burned-out area where there were so many bodies. Eventually, weeks later, she became ill but did not know until long after that it was radiation sickness. Murakami is a Japanese peace activist who has lectured at universities around the world. She currently writes for newspapers in Japan and visits many nations on peace pilgrimages.

SOURCE. Keiko Murakami, "My Hiroshima," Mary Lim's Adventures on the Land of the Rising Sun. http://mezza1.tripod.com/japan studentexchange/id13.html. Reproduced by permission.

It was a very hot day on August 6, 1945.

There was an air raid the night before, so everybody had to stay in shelters; nobody had a good sleep. That morning my father stayed home later than usual, and my mother was preparing breakfast. I casually said to my father that I did not want to go to school on that day. He was a very strict man, but strangely he gave me permission to cut classes. So I was inside, reading a magazine with my brother.

Suddenly father yelled from the yard, "I hear the plane!" My brother and I rushed outside. Father shouted, "Watch out! It's not the sound of a Japanese plane. Go into the shelter!" My brother and I jumped into the underground shelter.

The next instant, I felt a shock all over my body. At the same time, father jumped in with us. The three of us were buried under the collapsing house. I could see a tiny piece of sky form underneath the debris. My brother and I clung to my father's waist, and we crawled out. Because my father was one second too late getting into the shelter, he was badly wounded on the left side of his body. He tore a piece from my clothes and bound the wound tightly to stop the bleeding.

All the neighbouring houses were damaged. There was nothing left standing.

We yelled for my mother. Soon the heap of rubble moved, and she appeared with my baby sister in her arms. Many pieces of glass were stuck all over her body. Her right eyeball was out and drooped around her breast like a lump of blood. My father took off my mother's obi (waist sash), and used it to tie my sister on my back.

He held onto my mother and we started walking. We walked to the river about 300 metres away; during

> Wounded people were all around us, people badly hurt, people with their flesh melting and drooping because of the burns.

that time we saw nobody. It was dead silent as if we were the only ones left in the world.

Because we acted quickly, we seemed to be the first to come to the riverside. Father had my mother lie down in the shade of a bush. Before long, wounded people were all around us, people badly hurt, people with their flesh melting and drooping because of the burns. They were all crying and yelling. Their faces were so damaged by the heat of the blast that nobody could recognise anyone else. Probably it was only my brother and I who had no apparent injuries.

The Struggle to Survive

With water from the river, my father roughly washed my sister who was covered with my mother's blood. Thank God, she started breathing again. We thought she had suffocated. Father was wild with joy. But my mother's milk had stopped. When he dipped a piece of cloth into the water and tried to get my sister to suckle it, she just cried in a feeble voice. Something had to be done.

Then father found a woman who was squeezing the milk from her own breasts; he begged her to give her milk to my sister. She said, "My milk belongs to my child, who just passed away. I shall never give it to strangers." Father kneeled down on the ground and begged her again and again. Dying people around them also raised their voices saying, "Your dead baby will never come back, but you can save this living baby. Please give your milk to her." Finally, the woman collecting herself, offered to do just that, and my sister was saved.

On our side there was a well about 2 metres across. Wounded people peeped down into it. Having no means of scooping out the water, they ended up jumping into

> Having no means of scooping out the water, [the wounded] ended up jumping into the well one after another, until it became a heap of people. Many died of suffocation.

the well one after another, until it became a heap of people. Many died of suffocation. Some were still alive but could not move because of the many dead people on top of them. Within the same day, we were infested with maggots. They were creeping about not only on dead bodies, but also in living people's wounds.

There was a bad smell all over the place.

Father had a responsibility to help other citizens, and he tried to go to the [city] office to grasp the situation. Fires had started here and there; the river was filled with people and animals and furniture. Many people were gathering at the river to get water, so it was impossible for him to cross the river. Father gave up going to the office and decided to help the people around him. He announced that rescue would soon come, asked them to be patient, and tried to prevent rioting and plundering.

We could not fill our stomachs. I tried to eat cucumbers and eggplants which grew on the riverside, but spewed them out on the spot. After many years, I learned that those who ate them at that time died because of the radiation effects on the vegetables.

Soon, night fell. I could not sleep at all and kept watching the blazing flames. Towards daybreak the fires were under control, but it was a morning of unearthly quiet.

Mountain folds on the other side of the river showed no damage. My father's colleague lived in that area, so we thought if we could get there somehow we would be safe.

Father went back to the place where our house had been, and dug through the ruins left by the fire, finding a bottle of some pickled scallions and plums. On a piece of unburned wood he wrote, "The Murakami family are all alive. I am staying at the house of my colleague." He left the sign there so that anybody coming to search for us could see it.

My sister was fed by the woman once more. Father gave her the bottle of scallions and plums as a token of gratitude. I wonder what happened to her after she ate them, because I'm afraid that the pickles also had been affected by the radiation. After many years when things were settling down, we tried very hard to inquire after her, but [it was] in vain. We always remember her with agony, wondering if those pickles had taken her life.

I carried my sister on my back and took the arm of my brother. Father carried Mother on his back. Under a scorching sun, we started walking through the burnt out area with bare feet. The bottoms of our feet got burned and our skin stuck to the soil. Our pace was very slow. Always there was an emergency siren sounding.

"Mother seems very ill. I have to hurry on. Keiko, you come later," Father said to me. He put Mother into a baby carriage left on the road and started to run. I felt helpless but kept walking, trying very hard to protect my sister and brother.

The house we reached was full of people who had fled from the city. Father managed to find a space for Mother to lie down among those who were fatally injured. My brother and I had no place because we had no injury. We kept standing, with our backs against the wall.

In the evening of that day, we had the first meal after the bomb. It was a bowl of boiled water with a few pieces of vegetables and some grain. I dipped a piece of cloth in the soup and had my sister suckle it. The next day, Father's colleague got some skim milk from some-where. Father melted the milk powder with a lantern and fed my sister, but my brother and I had nothing more to eat.

Escaping from the Ruins of the City

My grandfather and uncle saw the notice on the ruins of our house and came looking for us. They explained, "It's said that a special bomb was dropped on Hiroshima."

Father had to stay to help the people. Mother was seriously injured, and my sister had to be with her. So, it was decided that my grandfather and uncle would take my brother and me to my grandfather's place.

Very early next morning we started walking. My brother and I had no clothes on and walked with our bare feet. We made a desperate effort to get through the area that had been burned out. I can still vividly remember what I saw that day.

> Under the crushed houses there were half burned bodies. Even with great effort not to step on the bodies, I did so many times.

The familiar sights were all gone. The burned out area went as far as my eyes could see. The water pipes were broken everywhere. Around those places, many dead bodies were piled on top of each other with lots of maggots on them. In hunger and thirst, they had come to at least have some water, and died. Under the crushed houses there were half burned bodies. Even with great effort not to step on the bodies, I did so many times. This memory is the one I shall have to carry all through my life. Even now, after more than 50 years, the soles of my feet ache when summer comes. . . .

We managed to walk for more than 50 kilometres, sometimes along the ridge of a cliff and other times through winding ravine, finally arriving at Grandfather's house at the end of the day. Already the family of my father's sister had arrived, having fled from the city like us.

Grandfather, as a shrine carpenter, had only a small piece of farmland. All the neighbouring farmers had their own relatives to support, so it was hard for us to get enough food. My brother and I were lonely without our parents, and we were always hungry. I had hard times to comfort my brother.

One day in early fall, suddenly I had a severe stomachache. There was blood in my urine and faeces. I shook all over with a high fever. The only doctor in town said, "It is dysentery. She must be kept in isolation." I was put in a dark storehouse. My hungry brother was crying outside, but I was forbidden by my grandmother and aunt from sharing my food with him. I was desperate. . . .

I did not receive any medical treatment, but just lay down for a month and became a little better, but before I knew it pus began oozing out of my ears, giving off a bad smell. The doctor said that it was because I was not keeping myself clean. So I took extra care to wash myself and wipe off the pus, but there was no sign of getting well. Somebody told me to apply the sap of the firewood, and I tried that, but my condition got worse.

It was not unreasonable that the doctors at that time diagnosed my illness as dysentery, since they had no knowledge about the A-Bomb. They didn't know until long afterwards that I was suffering from the after-effects of radioactivity.

Tending the Injured in the Aftermath of the Atomic Bombing

Johannes Siemes

In the following interview, Jesuit priest Johannes Siemes tells of seeing the explosion of the atomic bomb from a monastery in the foothills surrounding Hiroshima. He and his fellow priests treated the wounded who made their way there, then went down into the ruins of the city to rescue members of their order who were injured and unable to escape on their own. He describes the terrible destruction and the horror of being among the dead and dying he could not help. Siemes was a German priest with the Novitists of the Society of Jesus.

Up to August 6th [1945], occasional bombs, which did no great damage, had fallen on Hiroshima. Many cities roundabout, one after the other, were destroyed, but Hiroshima itself remained protected.

SOURCE. Johannes Siemes, "The Atomic Bombing of Hiroshima," *War Times Journal*. Reproduced by permission.

There were almost daily observation planes over the city but none of them dropped a bomb. The citizens wondered why they alone had remained undisturbed for so long a time. There were fantastic rumors that the enemy had something special in mind for this city, but no one dreamed that the end would come in such a fashion as on the morning of August 6th.

> " Suddenly . . . the whole valley is filled by a garish light which resembles the magnesium light used in photography. "

August 6th began in a bright, clear, summer morning. About 7 o'clock, there was an air raid alarm which we had heard almost every day and a few planes appeared over the city. No one paid attention and at about 8:00, the all-clear sounded. I am sitting in my room at the Novitists of the Society of Jesus in Nagatsuki . . . situated approximately 2 kilometers from Hiroshima, half-way up the side of a broad valley which stretches from the town at sea level into the mountainous hinterland, and through which courses a river. From my window, I have a wonderful view down the valley to the edge of the city. Suddenly—the time is approximately 8:15—the whole valley is filled by a garish light which resembles the magnesium light used in photography, and I am conscious of a wave heat. I jump to the window to find out the cause of this remarkable phenomenon, but I see nothing more than that brilliant yellow light. As I make for the door, it doesn't occur to me that the light might have something to do with enemy planes. On the way from the window, I hear a moderately loud explosion which seems to come from a distance and, at the same time, the windows are broken in with a loud crash. There has been an interval of perhaps ten seconds since the flash of light. I am sprayed by fragments of glass. The entire window frame has been forced into the room. I realize now that a bomb has burst and I am under the impression that it exploded directly over our house or in the immediate vicinity.

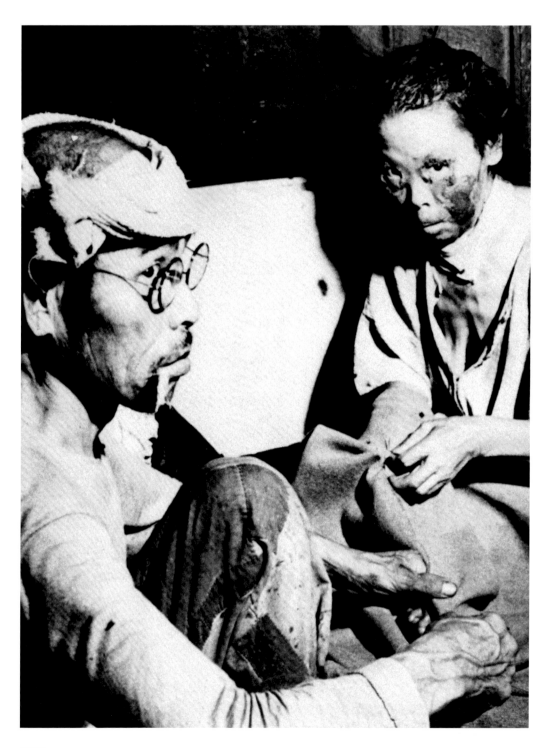

I am bleeding from cuts about the hands and head. I attempt to get out of the door. It has been forced outwards by the air pressure and has become jammed. I forced an opening in the door by means of repeated blows with my hands and feet and come to a broad hallway from which open the various rooms. Everything is in a state of confusion. All windows are broken and all the doors are forced inwards. The book-shelves in the hallway have tumbled down. I do not note a second explosion and the fliers seem to have gone on. A few are bleeding in the room, but none has been seriously injured. All of us have been fortunate since it is now apparent the wall of my room opposite the window has been lacerated by long fragments of glass.

We proceed to the front of the house to see where the bomb has landed. There is no evidence, however, of a bomb crater; but the southeast section of the house is severely damaged. Not a door nor a window remains. The blast of air had penetrated the entire house from the southeast, but the house still stands. It is constructed in the Japanese style with a wooden framework, but has been greatly strengthened by the labor of our Brother Gropper as is frequently done in Japanese homes. Only along the front of the chapel which adjoins the house have three supports given away (it has been made in the manner of a Japanese temple, entirely out of wood).

Down in the valley, perhaps one kilometer towards the city from us, several peasant homes are on fire and the woods on the opposite side of the valley are aflame. A few of us go over to help control the flames. While we are attempting to put things in order, a storm comes up and it begins to rain. Over the city, clouds of smoke are rising and I hear a few slight explosions. I come to the conclusion that an incendiary bomb with an especially strong explosive action has gone off down in the valley. A few of us saw three planes at great altitude over the city at the time of the explosion. I, myself, saw no aircraft whatsoever.

Photo on previous page: Two victims of the atomic bombings sit in a makeshift hospital. The woman's face was severely scarred by the tremendous heat generated by the explosion in Hiroshima. (**Associated Press.**)

Procession of the Wounded

Perhaps a half-hour after the explosion, a procession of people began to stream up the valley from the city. The crowd thickens continuously. A few come up the road to our house. Their steps are dragging. Many are bleeding or have suffered burns. We give them first aid and bring them into the chapel, which we have in the meantime cleaned and cleared of wreckage, and put them to rest on the straw mats which constitute the floor of Japanese houses. A few display horrible wounds of the extremities and back. The small quantity of fat which we possessed during this time was soon used up in the care of the burns. Father Nekter, who, before taking holy orders, had studied medicine, ministers to the injured, but our bandages and drugs are soon gone. We must be content with cleansing the wounds. More and more of the injured come to us. The least injured drag the more seriously wounded. There are wounded soldiers, and mothers carrying burned children in their arms. From the houses of the farmers in the valley comes word: "Our houses are full of wounded and dying. Can you help, at least by taking the worst cases?" The wounded come from the sections at the edge of the city. They saw the bright light, their houses collapsed and buried the inmates in their homes. Those that were in the open suffered instantaneous burns, particularly on the lightly clothed or unclothed parts of the body. Numerous fires spring up which soon consumed the entire district. We now conclude that the epicenter of the explosion was at the edge of the city near the Yokogawa Station, three kilometers away from us. . . .

Toward noon, our large chapel and library are filled with the seriously injured. The procession of refugees

> The wounded come from the sections at the edge of the city. They saw the bright light, their houses collapsed and buried the inmates in their homes.

from the city continues. Finally, about 1:00, Father Kepp returns together with the Sisters. Their house and the entire district where they live has burned to the ground. Father Kepp is bleeding about the head and neck, and he has a large burn on the right palm. He was standing in front of the nunnery ready to go home. All of a sudden, he became aware of the light, felt the wave of heat and a large blister formed on his hand. The windows were torn out by the blast. He thought that the bomb had fallen in his immediate vicinity. The nunnery, also a wooden structure made by our Brother Gropper, still remained but soon it was noted that the house is as good as lost because the fire, which began at many points in the neighborhood, sweeps closer and closer, and water is not available. There is still time to rescue certain things from the house and to bury them in an open spot. Then the house is swept by flame, and they fight their way back to us along the shore of the river and through the burning streets.

Rescue Mission

Soon comes news that the entire city has been destroyed by the explosion and that it is on fire. What became of Father Superior and the three other Brothers who were at the center of the city at the Central Mission and Parish House? We had up to this time not given them a thought because we did not believe that the effects of the bomb encompassed the entire city. Also, we did not want to go into town except under pressure of dire necessity, because we thought that the population was greatly perturbed and that it might take revenge on any foreigners whom they might consider spiteful onlookers of their misfortune, or even spies.

Brother Stolto and Brother Balighagen go down to the road which is still full of refugees and bring in the

> Where the city stood, there is a gigantic burned out sear.

seriously injured who have sunken by the wayside, to the temporary aid station at the village school. There, iodine is applied to the wounds but they are left uncleansed. Neither ointments nor other therapeutic agents are available. Those that have been brought in are laid on the floor and no one can give them any further care. What could one do when all means are lacking? Under these circumstances, it is almost useless to bring them in. Among the passersby, there are many who are uninjured. In a purposeless, insensate manner, distraught by the magnitude of the disaster, most of them rush by and none conceives the thought only with the welfare of their own families. It became clear to us during these days that the Japanese displayed little initiative, preparedness, and organizational skill in preparation for catastrophes. They despaired of any rescue work when something could have been saved by a cooperative effort, and fatalistically let the catastrophe take its course. When we urged them to take part in the rescue work, they did everything willingly, but on their own initiative they did very little.

At about 4:00 in the afternoon, a theology student and two kindergarten children, who lived at the Parish House in the city, came and reported that the church, Parish House and adjoining buildings had burned down, and that Father Superior, LaSalle and Father Schiffer had been seriously injured and that they had taken refuge in Asano Park on the river bank. It is obvious that we must bring them in since they are too weak to come here on foot.

Hurriedly, we get together two stretchers and seven of us rush toward the city. Father Rekter comes along with food and medicine. The closer we get to the city, the greater is the evidence of destruction and the more difficult it is to make our way. The houses at the edge of the city are all severely damaged. Many have collapsed or burned down. Further in, almost all of the dwellings have been damaged by fire. Where the city stood, there is a gigantic burned out sear. We make our way along the street on the river bank among the burning and smoking ruins. Twice we are forced into the river itself by the burning and smoking ruins. Twice we are forced into the river itself by the heat and smoke at the level of the street. Frightfully burned people beckon to us. Along the way, there are many dead and dying.

Entering the Destroyed City

On the Misasa Bridge, which leads into the inner city, we are met by a long procession of soldiers who have suffered burns. They drag themselves along with the help of staves or are carried by their less severely injured comrades . . . an endless procession of the unfortunate. Abandoned on the bridge, there stand with sunken heads a number of horses with large burns on their flanks. On the far side, the cement structure of the local hospital is the only building that remains standing. The interior, however, has been burned out. It acts as a landmark to guide us on our way. . . . Finally we reach the entrance of the park. A large proportion of the populace has taken refuge there, but even the trees of the park are on fire in several places. Paths and bridges are blocked by the trunks of fallen trees and are almost impassable. We are told that a high wind, which may well have resulted from the heat of the burning city, had uprooted the large trees. It is now quite dark. Only the fires which are still raging in some places at a distance, give out little light. At the far corner of the park, on the river bank itself, we at first come upon our colleagues. Father Schiffer is on the ground pale as a ghost. He has a deep incised wound behind his ear and has lost so much blood that we are concerned about his chances for survival. The Father Superior has suffered a deep wound of the lower leg. Father Cieslik and Father Kleinserge have minor injuries but are completely exhausted.

While they are eating the food that we have brought along, they tell us of their experiences. They were in their rooms at the Parish House—it was 8:15, exactly the time when we had heard the explosion in Nagatsuki—when came the intense light and immediately thereafter the sound of breaking windows, walls and furniture. They were showered with glass splinters and fragments of wreckage. Father Schiffer was buried beneath a portion of a wall and suffered a severe head injury. The Father Superior received most of the splinters in his back and lower extremity from which he bled copiously. Everything was thrown about in the rooms themselves, but the wooden framework of the house remained intact. The solidity of the structure that was the work of Brother Gropper again shown forth. They had the same impression that we had in Nagatsuki: that the bomb had burst in their immediate vicinity. The Church, school and all buildings in the immediate vicinity collapsed at once. Beneath the ruins of the school, the children cried for help. They were freed with great effort. Several others were also rescued from the ruins of nearby dwellings. Even the Father Superior and Father Schiffer, despite their wounds, rendered aid to others and lent a great deal of blood in the process. In the meantime, fires which had begun some distance away are raging even closer, so that it becomes obvious that everything would soon burn down. . . .

It is high time to flee, since the oncoming flames leave almost no way open. . . . Beneath the wreckage of the houses along the way, many have been trapped and they scream to be rescued from the oncoming flames. They must be left to face their fate.

> Many have been trapped and they scream to be rescued from the oncoming flames. They must be left to face their fate.

The Pilot of the *Enola Gay* Looks Back

Paul Tibbets, interviewed by Studs Terkel

In the following interview, which took place when he was eighty-seven years old, *Enola Gay* pilot Paul Tibbets recalls how he first heard about the atomic bomb, his experience as commander of the B-29 squadron that dropped it, and how he felt about the bombing of Hiroshima. He has had no second thoughts, he says, because the bombing saved many lives. Studs Terkel, the interviewer, was awarded the Pulitzer Prize for his book, *The Good War*, which contained ordinary people's reminiscences of World War II.

S tuds Terkel: *Once upon a time, you flew a plane called the* Enola Gay *over the city of Hiroshima, in Japan, on Sunday morning—August 6, 1945—and a bomb fell. It was the atomic bomb, the first ever. And that particular moment changed the whole world around. You were the pilot of that plane.*

Paul Tibbets: Yes, I was the pilot.

And the Enola Gay *was named after . . .*

My mother. She was Enola Gay Haggard before she married my dad, and my dad never supported me with the flying—he hated airplanes and motorcycles. When I told them I was going to leave college and go fly planes in the army air corps, my dad said, "Well, I've sent you through school, bought you automobiles, given you money to run around with the girls, but from here on, you're on your own. If you want to go kill yourself, go ahead, I don't give a damn." Then Mom just quietly said, "Paul, if you want to go fly airplanes, you're going to be all right." And that was that. . . .

> It was up to me now to put together an organization and train them to drop atomic weapons.

Now by 1944 you were a pilot—a test pilot on the program to develop the B-29 bomber. When did you get word that you had a special assignment?

One day [in September 1944] I'm running a test on a B-29, I land, a man meets me. He says he just got a call from General Uzal Ent [commander of the second air force] at Colorado Springs, he wants me in his office the next morning at nine o'clock. He said, "Bring your clothing—your B4 bag—because you're not coming back." Well, I didn't know what it was and didn't pay any attention to it—it was just another assignment. I got to Colorado Springs the next morning perfectly on time. A man named Lansdale met me, walked me to General Ent's office and closed the door behind me. With him was a man wearing a blue suit, a US Navy captain—that was William Parsons, who flew with me to Hiroshima—and Dr. Norman Ramsey, Columbia University professor in nuclear physics. And Norman said: "OK, we've got what we call the Manhattan Project. What we're doing is trying to develop an atomic bomb. We've gotten to the point now where we can't go much further till we have airplanes to work with."

He gave me an explanation which probably lasted 45, 50 minutes, and they left. General Ent looked at me and said, "The other day, General Arnold [commander general of the army air corps] offered me three names." Both of the others were full colonels; I was a lieutenant-colonel. He said that when General Arnold asked which of them could do this atomic weapons deal, he replied without hesitation, "Paul Tibbets is the man to do it." I said, "Well, thank you, sir." Then he laid out what was going on and it was up to me now to put together an organization and train them to drop atomic weapons. . . .

He said: "There's nobody could tell you what you have to do because nobody knows. If we can do anything to help you, ask me." I said thank you very much. He said, "Paul, be careful how you treat this responsibility, because if you're successful you'll probably be called a hero. And if you're unsuccessful, you might wind up in prison."

Preparing for the Mission

Did you know the power of an atomic bomb? Were you told about that?

No, I didn't know anything at that time. But I knew how to put an organization together. He said, "Go take a look at the bases, and call me back and tell me which one you want." I wanted to get back to Grand Island, Nebraska; that's where my wife and two kids were, where my laundry was done, and all that stuff. But I thought, "Well, I'll go to Wendover [army airfield, in Utah] first and see what they've got." As I came in over the hills I saw it was a beautiful spot. . . . This lieutenant-colonel in charge said, "We've just been advised to stop here and I don't know what you want to do . . . but if it has anything to do with this base, it's the most perfect base I've ever been on. You've got full machine shops, everybody's qualified, they know what they want to do. It's a good place."

And now you chose your own crew.

Well, I had mentally done it before that. I knew right away I was going to get Tom Ferebee [the *Enola Gay*'s bombardier] and Theodore "Dutch" van Kirk [navigator] and Wyatt Duzenbury [flight engineer].

Guys you had flown with in Europe?

Yeah.

And now you're training. And you're also talking to physicists like Robert Oppenheimer [senior scientist on the Manhattan project].

I think I went to Los Alamos [the Manhattan project HQ] three times, and each time I got to see Dr. Oppenheimer working in his own environment. . . .

Did Oppenheimer tell you about the destructive nature of the bomb?

No.

How did you know about that?

From Dr. Ramsey. He said the only thing we can tell you about it is, it's going to explode with the force of 20,000 tons of TNT. I'd never seen one pound of TNT blow up. I'd never heard of anybody who'd seen a hundred pounds of TNT blow up. All I felt was that this was gonna be one hell of a big bang.

Twenty thousand tons—that's equivalent to how many planes full of bombs?

Well, I think the two bombs that we used [at Hiroshima and Nagasaki] had more power than all the bombs the air force had used during the war in Europe.

So Ramsey told you about the possibilities.

Even though it was still theory, whatever those guys told me, that's what happened. So I was ready to say I wanted to go to war, but I wanted to ask Oppenheimer how to get away from the bomb after we dropped it. I told him that when we had dropped bombs in Europe and North Africa, we'd flown straight ahead after dropping them—which is also the trajectory of the bomb. But what should we do this time? He said, "You can't fly

Photo on following page: Colonel Paul Tibbets stands beside the B-29 bomber that dropped the atomic bomb on Hiroshima. The plane is named after his mother. (Associated Press.)

straight ahead because you'd be right over the top when it blows up and nobody would ever know you were there." He said I had to turn tangent to the expanding shock wave. I said, "Well, I've had some trigonometry, some physics. What is tangency in this case?" He said it was 159 degrees in either direction. "Turn 159 degrees as fast as you can and you'll be able to put yourself the greatest distance from where the bomb exploded."

How many seconds did you have to make that turn?

I had dropped enough practice bombs to realize that the charges would blow around 1,500 feet in the air, so I would have 40 to 42 seconds to turn 159 degrees. I went back to Wendover as quick as I could and took the airplane up. I got myself to 25,000 feet and I practiced turning, steeper, steeper, steeper and I got it where I could pull it round in 40 seconds. The tail was shaking dramatically and I was afraid of it breaking off, but I didn't quit. That was my goal. And I practiced and practiced until, without even thinking about it, I could do it in between 40 and 42, all the time. So, when that day came. . . .

Dropping the Bomb

You got the go-ahead on August 5.

Yeah. We were in Tinian [the US island base in the Pacific] at the time we got the OK. They had sent this Norwegian to the weather station out on Guam [the United State's westernmost territory] and I had a copy of his report. We said that, based on his forecast, the sixth day of August would be the best day that we could get over Honshu [the island on which Hiroshima stands]. So we did everything that had to be done to get the crews ready to go: airplane loaded, crews briefed, all of the things checked that you have to check before you can fly over enemy territory. . . . We were ready to go at about four o'clock in the afternoon on the fifth and we got word from the president that we were free to go. . . .

Well, we got going down the runway at right about 2:15 A.M. and we took off, we met our rendezvous guys, we made our flight up to what we call the initial point, that would be a geographic position that you could not mistake. Well, of course we had the best one in the world with the rivers and bridges and that big shrine. There was no mistaking what it was.

So you had to have the right navigator to get it on the button.

The airplane has a bomb sight connected to the autopilot and the bombardier puts figures in there for where he wants to be when he drops the weapon, and that's transmitted to the airplane. We always took into account what would happen if we had a failure and the bomb bay doors didn't open; we had a manual release put in each airplane so it was right down by the bombardier and he could pull on that. And the guys in the airplanes that followed us to drop the instruments needed to know when it was going to go. We were told not to use the radio, but, hell, I had to. I told them I would say, "One minute out," "Thirty seconds out," "Twenty seconds" and "Ten" and then I'd count, "Nine, eight, seven, six, five, four seconds," which would give them a time to drop their cargo. They knew what was going on because they knew where we were. And that's exactly the way it worked; it was absolutely perfect. After we got the airplanes in formation I crawled into the tunnel and went back to tell the men, I said, "You know what we're doing today?" They said, "Well, yeah, we're going on a bombing mission." I said, "Yeah, we're going on a bombing mission, but it's a little bit special." My tail gunner, Bob [George R.] Caron, was pretty alert. He said, "Colonel, we wouldn't be playing

> When I level out, the nose is a little bit high and as I look up there the whole sky is lit up in the prettiest blues and pinks I've ever seen in my life.

> I had accelerometers installed in all airplanes to record the magnitude of the bomb. It hit us with two and a half G.

with atoms today, would we?" I said, "Bob, you've got it just exactly right."

So I went back up in the front end and I told the navigator, bombardier, flight engineer, in turn. I said, "OK, this is an atom bomb we're dropping." They listened intently but I didn't see any change in their faces or anything else. Those guys were no idiots. We'd been fiddling round with the most peculiar-shaped things we'd ever seen. So we're coming down. We get to that point where I say "one second" and by the time I'd got that second out of my mouth the airplane had lurched, because 10,000 pounds had come out of the front. I'm in this turn now, tight as I can get it, that helps me hold my altitude and helps me hold my airspeed and everything else all the way round. When I level out, the nose is a little bit high and as I look up there the whole sky is lit up in the prettiest blues and pinks I've ever seen in my life. It was just great. . . .

Did you hear an explosion?

Oh yeah. The shockwave was coming up at us after we turned. And the tail gunner said, "Here it comes." About the time he said that, we got this kick in the ass. I had accelerometers installed in all airplanes to record the magnitude of the bomb. It hit us with two and a half G [a measure of gravitational force]. Next day, when we got figures from the scientists on what they had learned from all the things, they said, "When that bomb exploded, your airplane was ten and half miles away from it."

Did you see that mushroom cloud?

You see all kinds of mushroom clouds, but they were made with different types of bombs. The Hiroshima bomb did not make a mushroom. It was what I call a stringer. It just came up. It was black as hell and it had light and colors and white in it and grey color in it and the top was like a folded-up Christmas tree.

Do you have any idea what happened down below?

Pandemonium! I think it's best stated by one of the historians, who said: "In one micro-second, the city of Hiroshima didn't exist." . . .

No Second Thoughts

Do you ever have any second thoughts about the bomb?

Second thoughts? No. Studs, look. Number one, I got into the air corps to defend the United States to the best of my ability. That's what I believe in and that's what I work for. Number two, I'd had so much experience with airplanes. I'd had jobs where there was no particular direction about how you do it and then of course I put this thing together with my own thoughts on how it should be because when I got the directive I was to be self-supporting at all times. On the way to the target I was thinking: I can't think of any mistakes I've made. Maybe I did make a mistake: maybe I was too damned assured. At 29 years of age I was so shot in the ass with confidence I didn't think there was anything I couldn't do. Of course, that applied to airplanes and people. So, no, I had no problem with it. I knew we did the right thing because when I knew we'd be doing that I thought, yes, we're going to kill a lot of people, but by God we're going to save a lot of lives. We won't have to invade [Japan].

> I knew we did the right thing because . . . I thought, yes, we're going to kill a lot of people, but by God we're going to save a lot of lives.

Why did they drop the second one, the Bockscar [bomb] on Nagasaki?

Unknown to anybody else—I knew it, but nobody else knew—there was a third one. See, the first bomb went off and they didn't hear anything out of the Japanese for two or three days. The second bomb was dropped and again they were silent for another couple of days. Then I got a phone call from General Curtis LeMay [chief of staff of the strategic air forces in the Pacific]. He said, "You got another one of those damn things?" I said, "Yes sir." He said, "Where is it?" I said, "Over in Utah." He said, "Get it out here. You and your crew are going to fly it." I said, "Yes sir." I sent word back and the crew loaded it on an airplane and we headed back to bring it right on out to Tinian and when they got it to California debarkation point, the war was over.

Opposing the Atomic Bomb as a Teen in 1945

Daniel Ellsberg

In the following viewpoint, Daniel Ellsberg tells how he felt on hearing the announcement of the bombing of Hiroshima when he was fourteen years old. Unlike most people, he had heard of atomic bombs before, in a ninth-grade class where the teacher discussed scientific speculation about them (not knowing that one was really being developed) and asked the students to write papers about the implications of such a bomb were it to be made. He and his classmates had concluded that an atomic bomb would be very bad for humanity, so he could not share the positive view of most other Americans about the news. He believed—as he still does—that the nation's leaders were immoral and untrustworthy. Ellsberg is a political activist best known for leaking the secret "Pentagon Papers" to the press during the Vietnam War, an act that had far-reaching consequences. He is the author of several books.

SOURCE. Daniel Ellsberg, "Hiroshima Day: America Has Been Asleep at the Wheel for 64 Years," www.ellsberg.net, 2009. Reproduced by permission.

It was a hot August day in Detroit. I was standing on a street corner downtown, looking at the front page of the *Detroit News* in a news rack. I remember a streetcar rattling by on the tracks as I read the headline: A single American bomb had destroyed a Japanese city. My first thought was that I knew exactly what that bomb was. It was the U-235 bomb we had discussed in school and written papers about the previous fall.

I thought: "We got it first. And we used it. On a city."

> I had a sense of dread . . . a feeling, new to me as an American, at [age] 14, that my country might have made a terrible mistake.

I had a sense of dread, a feeling that something very ominous for humanity had just happened. A feeling, new to me as an American, at 14, that my country might have made a terrible mistake. I was glad when the war ended nine days later, but it didn't make me think that my first reaction on Aug. 6 was wrong.

Unlike nearly everyone else outside the Manhattan Project, my first awareness of the challenges of the nuclear era had occurred—and my attitudes toward the advent of nuclear weaponry had formed—some nine months earlier than those headlines, and in a crucially different context.

An Unusual School Assignment

It was in a ninth-grade social studies class in the fall of 1944. I was 13, a boarding student on full scholarship at Cranbrook, a private school in Bloomfield Hills, Mich. Our teacher, Bradley Patterson, was discussing a concept that was familiar then in sociology, William F. Ogburn's notion of "cultural lag."

The idea was that the development of technology regularly moved much further and faster in human social-historical evolution than other aspects of culture: our institutions of government, our values, habits, our understanding of society and ourselves. Indeed, the very notion of "progress" referred mainly to technology. What "lagged" behind, what developed more slowly or not at all in social adaptation to new technology was everything that bore on our ability to *control* and direct technology and the use of technology to dominate other humans.

To illustrate this, Mr. Patterson posed a potential advance in technology that might be realized soon. It was possible now, he told us, to conceive of a bomb made of U-235, an isotope of uranium, which would have an explosive power 1,000 times greater than the largest bombs being used in the war that was then going on. German scientists in late 1938 had discovered that uranium could be split by nuclear fission, in a way that would release immense amounts of energy.

Several popular articles about the possibility of atomic bombs and specifically U-235 bombs appeared during the war in magazines like the *Saturday Evening Post*. None of these represented leaks from the Manhattan Project, whose very existence was top-secret. In every case they had been inspired by earlier articles on the subject that had been published freely in 1939 and 1940, before scientific self-censorship and then formal classification had set in. Patterson had come across one of these wartime articles. He brought the potential development to us as an example of one more possible leap by science and technology ahead of our social institutions.

Suppose, then, that one nation, or several, chose to explore the possibility of making this into a bomb, and succeeded. What would be the probable implications of this for humanity? How would it be used, by humans and states as they were today? Would it be, on balance, bad or good for the world? Would it be a force for peace, for example, or for destruction? We were to write a short essay on this, within a week.

I recall the conclusions I came to in my paper after thinking about it for a few days. As I remember, everyone

Daniel Ellsberg, who knew about the destructive potential of atomic fission before the Hiroshima bombing, expressed opposition to such an act even before it happened. (**Associated Press.**)

in the class had arrived at much the same judgment. It seemed pretty obvious.

The existence of such a bomb—we each concluded—would be bad news for humanity. Mankind could not handle such a destructive force. It could not control it, safely, appropriately. The power would be "abused": used dangerously and destructively, with terrible consequences. Many cities would be destroyed entirely, just as the Allies were doing their best to destroy German cities without atomic bombs at that very time, just as the Germans earlier had attempted to do to Rotterdam and London. Civilization, perhaps our species, would be in danger of destruction.

It was just too powerful. Bad enough that bombs already existed that could destroy a whole city block. They were called "block-busters": 10 tons of high explosive. Humanity didn't need the prospect of bombs a thousand times more powerful, bombs that could destroy whole cities.

As I recall, this conclusion didn't depend mainly on who had the Bomb, or how many had it, or who got it first. And to the best of my memory, we in the class weren't addressing it as something that might come so soon as to bear on the outcome of the ongoing war. It seemed likely, the way the case was presented to us, that the Germans would get it first, since they had done the original science. But we didn't base our negative assessment on the idea that this would necessarily be a Nazi or German bomb. It would be a bad development, on balance, even if democratic countries got it first.

> I was put off by the lack of concern in [President Truman's] voice, the absence of a sense of tragedy, of desperation or fear for the future.

Disturbing Feelings

After we turned in our papers and discussed them in class, it was months before I thought of the issues again.

I remember the moment when I did, on a street corner in Detroit. I can still see and feel the scene and recall my thoughts, described above, as I read the headline on Aug. 6.

I remember that I was uneasy, on that first day and in the days ahead, about the tone in President Harry Truman's voice on the radio as he exulted over our success in the race for the Bomb and its effectiveness against Japan. I generally admired Truman, then and later, but in hearing his announcements I was put off by the lack of concern in his voice, the absence of a sense of tragedy, of desperation or fear for the future. It seemed to me that this was a decision best made in anguish; and both Truman's manner and the tone of the official communiqués made unmistakably clear that this hadn't been the case.

> Such feelings—about our president, and our Bomb—separated me from nearly everyone around me.

Which meant for me that our leaders didn't have the picture, didn't grasp the significance of the precedent they had set and the sinister implications for the future. And that evident unawareness was itself scary. I believed that something ominous had happened; that it was bad for humanity that the Bomb was feasible, and that its use would have bad long-term consequences, whether or not those negatives were balanced or even outweighed by short-run benefits.

Looking back, it seems clear to me my reactions then were right. . . .

I sensed almost right away, in August 1945 as Hiroshima and Nagasaki were incinerated, that such feelings—about our president, and our Bomb—separated me from nearly everyone around me, from my parents and friends and from most other Americans. They were not to be mentioned. They could only sound unpatriotic. And in World War II, that was about the last way one wanted to sound. These were thoughts to be kept to myself.

Unlikely thoughts for a 14-year-old American boy to have had the week the war ended? Yes, if he hadn't been in Mr. Patterson's social studies class the previous fall. Every member of that class must have had the same flash of recognition of the Bomb as they read the August headlines during our summer vacation. Beyond that, I don't know whether they responded as I did, in the terms of our earlier discussion.

But neither our conclusions then or reactions like mine on Aug. 6 stamped us as gifted prophets. Before that day perhaps no one in the public outside our class—no one else outside the Manhattan Project (and very few inside it)—had spent a week, as we had, or even a day thinking about the impact of such a weapon on the long-run prospects for humanity.

Apart from Other Americans

And we were set apart from our fellow Americans in another important way. Perhaps no others outside the project or our class *ever* had occasion to think about the Bomb without the strongly biasing positive associations that accompanied their first awareness in August 1945 of its very possibility: that it was "our" weapon, an instrument of American democracy developed to deter a Nazi Bomb, pursued by two presidents, a war-winning weapon and a necessary one—so it was claimed and almost universally believed—to end the war without a costly invasion of Japan.

Unlike nearly all the others who started thinking about the new nuclear era after Aug. 6, our attitudes of the previous fall had not been shaped, or warped, by the claim and appearance that such a weapon had just won a war for the forces of justice, a feat that supposedly would otherwise have cost a million American lives (and as many or more Japanese).

For nearly all other Americans, whatever dread they may have felt about the long-run future of the Bomb (and there was more expression of this in elite media than most people remembered later) was offset at the time and ever afterward by a powerful aura of its legitimacy, and its almost miraculous potential for good which had already been realized. For a great many Americans still, the Hiroshima and Nagasaki bombs are regarded above all with *gratitude*, for having saved their own lives or the lives of their husbands, brothers, fathers or grandfathers, which would otherwise have been at risk in the invasion of Japan. For these Americans and many others, the Bomb was not so much an instrument of massacre as a kind of savior, a protector of precious lives.

Most Americans ever since have seen the destruction of the populations of Hiroshima and Nagasaki as necessary and effective—as constituting just means, in effect just terrorism, under the supposed circumstances—thus legitimating, in their eyes, the second and third largest single-day massacres in history. (The largest, also by the U.S. Army Air Corps, was the firebombing of Tokyo five months before on the night of March 9, which burned alive or suffocated 80,000 to 120,000 civilians. Most of the very few Americans who are aware of this event at all accept it, too, as appropriate in wartime.)

To regard those acts as definitely other than criminal and immoral—as most Americans do—is to believe that anything—*anything*—can be legitimate means: at worst, a necessary, lesser, evil. At least, if done by Americans, on the order of a president, during wartime. Indeed, we are the only country in the world that believes it won a war by bombing—specifically by bombing cities with weapons of mass destruction—and believes that it was fully rightful in doing so. It is a dangerous state of mind.

Gratitude for the Atomic Bomb that Ended the War

Bob Greene

In the following viewpoint, Bob Greene quotes from the responses he received after writing a newspaper article about his interview with Paul Tibbets, the pilot of the plane that dropped the first atomic bomb. Many people wrote to tell him that the use of the bomb saved their lives or the lives of their families, including children who otherwise would never have been born. Greene, an award-winning columnist for the *Chicago Tribune*, is the author of many books.

E very day, my computer at work was jammed with electronic messages about the interview with [*Enola Gay* pilot Paul] Tibbets; regular mail also poured in, and phone calls. That one three-sentence

SOURCE. Bob Greene, *Duty: A Father, His Son, and the Man Who Won the War*. Copyright © 2000 by Bob Greene. Reproduced by permission of HarperCollins Publishers.

thought of Tibbets'—"I cannot communicate with people who are less than sixty years old. It's as if all of us in this country know the same words, but we don't use the words the same way. We speak different languages."—seemed to affect people. Some were his age, some weren't, but all understood what he meant. And they wanted to say so.

The most overwhelming sentiment in so many of the letters concerned something I had not thought much about before I had met Tibbets. It was about the lives that were *not* lost when the bomb was dropped; it was about the American families that were allowed to be born and thrive and grow to adulthood because the soldiers and sailors had not been sent on a bloody and disastrous land invasion of Japan.

Voices:

"At the time of Colonel Paul Tibbets' mission, I was a young nineteen-year-old Marine," wrote a man named Robert A. Guth.

> We had just finished some intense training for the final push against the Japanese homeland. Although our exact invasion location was secret, we found out later that we would indeed be sent in. At that time we heard scuttle-butt that an invasion of Japan would be very costly in casualties. I would have liked to thank President Truman at that time for his decision to order the bombing—and I would like at this time to thank Paul Tibbets for his excellent mission.
>
> I thank Colonel Tibbets and his crew, my wife Mary thanks them, our five children and fifteen grandchildren thank them.

It was an expression of gratitude that I would read and hear over and over. The point was unmistakable—so many people, most of them of Tibbets' and my father's generation, were absolutely convinced that untold numbers of American lives, including perhaps their own, would have soon been lost had Tibbets and his crew not flown their mission in August of 1945. These correspondents did not treat what happened in Hiroshima lightly; far from it, they made it clear that they understood in great detail the unfathomable extent of death and carnage that resulted from the bomb being dropped.

But they also seemed to feel that the bomb—in a complex and pervading sense—was their salvation, and the salvation of family members not yet born in 1945.

"Younger Generations Cannot Possibly Understand What We Went Through"

A woman named Catherine E. Mitchell, seventy-three years old, of Biloxi, Mississippi, put it this way:

I well remember that day when the bomb was dropped on Hiroshima. So often I have heard people saying that we should never have dropped that bomb. But those people were not living through the war.

In early 1945, my husband was sent to the Pacific. The country was preparing for the invasion of Japan and we all knew it. Had the dropping of the bomb not happened, I know that my husband would not have returned home—so many American lives would have been lost.

The younger generations cannot possibly understand what we went through and how we felt about our country being attacked [at Pearl Harbor]—you can't know until you live through it. My forty-six-year-old father was also in the Pacific with the Seabees then, and my twenty-year-old brother was finishing flight training.

I sincerely hope that the young people of today will never have to go through a war. I am glad that I did not have to make the decision [to drop the bomb], but I am glad that it was done.

> 'So often I have heard people saying that we should never have dropped that bomb. But those people were not living through the war.'

From a man named E. R. Klamm:

I was a naval communications officer, and we headed a large convoy of ships in Guam, Tinian and Saipan for the eventual invasion of Japan. We weathered three different typhoons.

In August, during a lull in the weather, I was playing badminton on deck (staying fit) when a staffman brought me a communication. I read it and then resumed playing our game. Then, like a bolt of lightning, I suddenly returned to the communication.

Its wording was technical and complex, but I interpreted that it involved the use of a mega-explosive in bombing Japan. It triggered in my mind that it could stop the invasion of Japan. Hallelujah! Hallelujah! Later aboard ship there was jubilation.

We never reached Japan. We did go to Korea and China. I then returned to the U.S. and the happiness of family life. I commend Paul Tibbets and his crew. I congratulate him for naming his B-29 the *Enola Gay*, in honor of his mother. *My* mother, and my wife, were happy on my return Thanksgiving Day, 1945.

From a twenty-five-year-old woman named Chantal Foster Lindquist:

Paul Tibbets' voice is stern and serene. The gravity of his act forces silence on the page.

I think most people my age don't understand the sacrifices our grandparents made during wartime. I remember, in high school, I wrote a paper about why we shouldn't have dropped the bomb on Hiroshima. I was adamant in my essay, but the moment I spoke with my grandfather, a Navy Seabee, and listened to his account of the war, I changed my mind.

His blue eyes flared when I said the bomb was unnecessary, and he leaned across the table to tell me how the bomb had saved his life. How he was so grateful to go home and see his family again. How he's pretty sure he would have been killed otherwise. And so in a way I realized I might not even be here if Paul Tibbets hadn't done his job.

A Perspective Born of the War

Some of the letters were filled with a perspective that could be born only of that war and that time. From a "septuagenarian ex-city editor" named Brad Bradford:

You quite properly focus upon the *Enola Gay*'s pilot. His command responsibilities must have been enormous.

But please bear with me. . . . To bring the *Enola Gay* over target within seventeen seconds of the planned time, navigator Theodore Van Kirk had to have been virtually perfect with no chance to relax even for a minute on that two-thousand-mile run to Hiroshima. His was simply an almost miraculous exhibition of technical expertise.

I was a B-29 navigator in Stateside training that August. Training that summer at Smoky Hill Army Airfield in Kansas, I was slated to head for the Pacific and fly cover for a land invasion of Japan. The Air Corps shipped my footlocker to Okinawa, but thanks to the flight of the *Enola Gay*, the Army decided it didn't need me there after all and returned it to Smoky Hill. I left active duty that December a Stateside-safeside WWII veteran. And I still have that footlocker as a reminder of the debt I owe Paul Tibbets and his crew.

There it was, in almost every letter—a legacy of the flight that was seldom spoken about publicly. One woman's words:

My husband was with the 5th Marine Division and served on Iwo Jima. After the *Enola Gay* dropped the bomb on Hiroshima, my husband and the men he fought with did not have to invade the Japanese mainland. He came home to me instead.

Ten years ago, my husband went into the bedroom to take a nap before dinner. When I went in to call him, he was dead. He was a wonderful husband and father, and our lives are very empty without him.

I am writing to ask you if I could possibly have Mr. Tibbets' address. I would really love to write to him. I am aware [that he] remains out of the public eye. But maybe he would like to hear about the special man I shared my life with—because of the job he did.

CHRONOLOGY

1939   August 2: Physicist Albert Einstein sends a letter to US President Franklin D. Roosevelt advising him that Nazi Germany may be trying to develop an atomic bomb and suggesting that the United States should begin its own research to prevent the Nazis from getting the weapon first.

October 11: Roosevelt authorizes the creation of the Advisory Committee on Uranium, the first step in a research project on the release of atomic energy.

1941   October 9: Roosevelt authorizes development of an atomic bomb.

December 7: The Japanese attack Pearl Harbor and the United States declares war against Japan. Four days later, Germany declares war on the United States.

1942   August 13: The Manhattan Engineer District (MED), whose task becomes known as the Manhattan Project, is established by the US Army to study the design of an atomic bomb. Contrary to common belief, "Manhattan" is not a code name, but simply indicates the location of the initial headquarters. During the next few months, other sites are chosen for future work.

1943   April 5: Research begins at Los Alamos, New Mexico, where the bomb is to be built.

1944   December 9: The 509th Composite Group of the US Army Air Force, based at Wendover, Utah, is formed under the command of Lieutenant Colonel Paul Tibbets and begins training to deliver the bomb.

1945   March 9–10: The firebombing of Tokyo results in more than 100,000 casualties in a single night.

April 12: Roosevelt dies and Harry S. Truman becomes president. The next day he is told about the Manhattan Project, the existence of which was not revealed to him while he was vice president.

April 27: The Target Committee of the Manhattan Project begins meeting to select possible targets for the atomic bomb.

May: The list of potential targets in Japan is narrowed down to Kyoto, Hiroshima, Yokohama, and Kokura; then Niigata replaces Yokohama and the Secretary of War rules out Kyoto because of its historic and cultural importance. Nagasaki is added later.

May 7: Germany surrenders to the Allied powers, ending World War II in Europe.

May 31: The Interim Committee of the War Department meets to make recommendations on the use of atomic weapons, international regulation of information, and domestic control of atomic energy.

June 6: The Interim Committee recommends that the bomb be kept secret and used as soon as possible without warning.

June 21: The Interim Committee rejects a report from scientists advocating international control of atomic research and proposing a demonstration of the atomic bomb prior to its use.

July 1: Physicist Leo Szilard begins a petition from scientists asking President Truman to call off using the atomic bomb against Japan.

July 14: Parts of the uranium bomb are sent by ship from San Francisco to Tinian Island in the Pacific, where they are to be assembled.

July 16: The first nuclear explosion in history occurs when a plutonium bomb, known by the code name "The Gadget," is tested at the Alamogordo Bombing Range near Los Alamos, New Mexico. The test is code-named "Trinity," and the date is thereafter considered the beginning of the Atomic Age.

July 17–August 2: Truman confers at Potsdam, Germany, with British prime minister Winston Churchill and Soviet premier Joseph Stalin to decide how to administer occupied Germany. Churchill knows about the atomic bomb because the British participated in the Manhattan Project.

July 24: Truman informs Russian leader Joseph Stalin about the bomb; Stalin has already found out about it through espionage, however.

July 25: President Truman authorizes the Army Air Force to use the bomb as soon after August 3 as weather permits.

July 26: Truman, Chinese president Chiang Kai-Shek, and new British prime minister Clement Atlee issue the Potsdam Proclamation, calling for Japan to surrender unconditionally.

The bomb arrives at Tinian, where B-29 crews are flying practice missions.

August 6: A uranium bomb called "Little Boy" is dropped on Hiroshima by the B-29 *Enola Gay*, piloted by Colonel Tibbets.

The attack on Hiroshima is announced to the nation and to the world in a White House press release prepared by Truman while aboard a ship returning from Potsdam.

August 8: Millions of leaflets are dropped by the United States on Japanese cities warning civilians to evacuate. The Soviet Union declares war on Japan and invades Manchuria.

August 9: A plutonium bomb called "Fat Man" is dropped on Nagasaki by the B-29 *Bockscar* (sometimes spelled *Bock's Car*), piloted by Major Charles W. Sweeney. The primary target had been Kokura, which was obscured by smoke and haze.

President Truman gives a radio address to the nation in which he again warns Japan that there will be more atomic bombings if they do not surrender.

August 10: Japanese civilian and military leaders fail to reach agreement, and Emperor Hirohito, breaking with tradition, intervenes. He instructs negotiators to surrender provided he will be allowed to keep his position.

August 13: Truman orders the resumption of conventional firebombing, and the largest raid of the war, involving more than a thousand B-29s and other aircraft, is launched.

August 14: The emperor orders acceptance of the Allies' terms and records a speech announcing surrender. Military leaders attempt to destroy the recording, but it is smuggled out of the palace.

Truman announces Japan's surrender.

The emperor's speech is broadcast (August 15 Japan time) to the Japanese people, who are stunned by the news.

September 2: The Japanese sign articles of surrender in a formal ceremony aboard the USS *Missouri*. President Truman again addresses the nation by radio, proclaiming this VJ (Victory over Japan) Day.

1946   August 1: President Truman signs the Atomic Energy Act, which establishes the Atomic Energy Commission to control atomic weapons and atomic power.

August 31: An entire issue of the prominent magazine *The New Yorker* is devoted to an article describing the experiences of six survivors of the Hiroshima bombing. These are the first detailed survivor stories Americans have seen and are widely circulated, eventually in book form.

1949   August 6: The Hiroshima Peace Memorial City Construction Law is passed in Japan, aimed at "the construction of Hiroshima as a Peace Memorial City, a symbol of the ideal of making lasting peace a reality."

1951   September 8: The San Francisco Peace Treaty is signed, ending Allied occupation of Japan as of April 1952. This also ends censorship of the Japanese press with regard to the details of the Hiroshima and Nagasaki bombings and their aftermath, but many earlier films were not declassified until years later.

1954   April 1: The Hiroshima Peace Memorial Park, built on an open field created in the center of the city by the bombing, is opened. Today it draws more than a million visitors annually.

1955   August 24: The Hiroshima Peace Memorial Museum opens, with exhibits presenting the facts of the bombing and advocating the banning of nuclear weapons throughout the world. It is now a popular destination for school field trips and international visitors.

1994   May 23: The American Legion formally protests the plan of the Air and Space Museum at the Smithsonian Institution to exhibit the *Enola Gay* and memorabilia from its crew in a context implying that the United States was in the wrong for the atomic bombing of Japan. Congress and many other veterans' groups join the protest, which is widely covered by the media.

1995   January 30: The planned exhibit of the *Enola Gay* is cancelled. A modified display including the plane's fuselage is exhibited later that year.

2003   December 15: The Smithsonian's Air and Space Museum puts the fully restored *Enola Gay* on permanent display.

2010   August 6: For the first time, the United States sends an official envoy to the annual ceremony in Hiroshima marking the anniversary (in this case, the sixty-fifth) of the city's destruction by the atomic bomb.

FOR FURTHER READING

Books

Rodney Barker, *The Hiroshima Maidens: A Story of Courage, Compassion and Survival.* New York: Viking, 1985.

Al Christman, *Target Hiroshima: Deak Parsons and the Creation of the Atomic Bomb.* Annapolis, MD: Naval Institute Press, 1998.

Leslie Groves, *Now It Can Be Told.* New York: Harper, 1962.

Michihiko Hachiya, *Hiroshima Diary: The Journal of a Japanese Physician, August 6–September 30, 1945.* Chapel Hill: University of North Carolina Press, 1995.

John Hersey, *Hiroshima.* New York: Knopf, 1946.

Michael J. Hogan, ed., *Hiroshima in History and Memory.* New York: Cambridge University Press, 1996.

Cynthia C. Kelly, ed., *The Manhattan Project: The Birth of the Atomic Bomb in the Words of Its Creators, Eyewitnesses and Historians.* New York: Black Dog & Leventhal, 2007.

Robert Jay Lifton, *Death in Life: Survivors of Hiroshima.* Chapel Hill: University of North Carolina Press, 1991.

Robert Jay Lifton and Greg Mitchell, *Hiroshima in America.* New York: Putnam, 1995.

Robert James Maddox, *Hiroshima in History: The Myths of Revisionism.* Columbia: University of Missouri Press, 2007.

Robert P. Newman, *Enola Gay and the Court of History.* New York: Peter Land, 2004.

Charles T. O'Reilly and William A. Rooney, *Enola Gay and the Smithsonian Institution.* Jefferson, NC: MacFarland, 2005.

Richard Rhodes, *The Making of the Atomic Bomb.* New York: Simon and Schuster, 1995.

Gaynor Sekimori, *Hibakusha: Survivors of Hiroshima and Nagasaki*. Tokyo: Kosei Publishing Co., 1986.

Martin Sherwin, *A World Destroyed: Hiroshima and Its Legacies*. Palo Alto, CA: Stanford University Press, 2003.

Henry Lewis Stimson, *The Decision to Use the Atomic Bomb*. New York: Harper, 1947.

Charles W. Sweeney, *War's End: An Eyewitness Account of America's Last Atomic Mission*. New York: Avon, 1997.

Ronald Takaki, *Hiroshima: Why America Dropped the Atomic Bomb*. Boston: Little, Brown, 1995.

Paul W. Tibbets, *Flight of the Enola Gay*. Reynoldsburg, OH: Buckeye Aviation Book Co., 1989.

———, *Return of the Enola Gay*. Columbus, OH: Mid Coast Marketing, 1998.

Dennis D. Wainstock, *The Decision to Drop the Atomic Bomb*. Westport, CT: Praeger, 1996.

J. Samuel Walker, *Prompt and Utter Destruction: Truman and the Use of Atomic Bombs Against Japan*. Chapel Hill: University of North Carolina Press, 2004.

Stephen Walker, *Shockwave: Countdown to Hiroshima*. New York: HarperCollins, 2005.

George Weller, *First Into Nagasaki: The Censored Eyewitness Dispatches on Post-Atomic Japan and Its Prisoners of War*. New York: Crown, 2006.

Periodicals

Gar Alperovitz, "Why the United States Dropped the Bomb," *Technology Review*, August-September, 1995.

Peter Blute, "Revisionist History Has Few Defenders," *Technology Review*, August-September, 1995.

Paul D. Boyer, "The Cloud Over the Culture: How Americans Imagined the Bomb They Dropped," *New Republic*, August 12, 1985.

William F. Buckley, Jr., "Hiroshima—Happy Birthday?" *National Review*, August 28, 1995.

Karl T. Compton, "If the Atomic Bomb Had Not Been Used," *Atlantic Monthly*, December 1946.

Robert DeVore, "What the Atomic Bomb Really Did," *Collier's*, March 2, 1946.

John W. Dower, "Hiroshima, Nagasaki, and the Politics of Memory," *Technology Review*, August-September, 1995.

Martin Fackler, "At Hiroshima Ceremony, a First for a U.S. Envoy," *New York Times*, August 6, 2010.

Richard B. Frank, "Why Truman Dropped the Bomb," *Weekly Standard*, August 8, 2005.

Benedict Giamo, "The Myth of the Vanquished: The Hiroshima Peace Memorial Museum," *American Quarterly*, December 2003.

D.M. Giangreco, "Harry Truman and the Price of Victory: New Light on the President's Biggest Decision," *American Heritage*, May 2003.

Paul Gray, "Doomsdays," *Time*, August 7, 1995.

Robert Guillain, "I Thought My Last Hour Had Come," *Atlantic Monthly*, August 1980.

John Hersey, "Hiroshima," *New Yorker*, August 31, 1946.

John Hersey and Roger Angell, "The Day the Bomb Fell," *New Yorker*, July 31, 1995.

I.B. Holley, Jr., "Second-Guessing History," *Technology Review*, August-September, 1995.

Walter Isaacson, "Why Did We Drop the Bomb?" *Time*, August 19, 1985.

Satoshi Kanazawa, "Dropping Atomic Bombs on Japan Was an Act of Utmost Compassion," *Psychology Today* blog, August 21, 2008. www.psychologytoday.com/blog/the-scientific-fundamentalist.

Michael B. King, "Shock Treatment: Horrible As The Destruction at Hiroshima and Nagasaki Was, a Continuing War Would Have Been Far Worse," *National Review*, April 3, 1995.

Nicholas D. Kristof, "Blood on Our Hands?" *New York Times*, August 3, 2005.

Robert Jay Lifton and Greg Mitchell, "The Age of Numbing," *Technology Review*, August-September, 1995.

Robert James Maddox, "The Biggest Decision: Why We Had to Drop the Atomic Bomb," *American Heritage*, May-June 1995.

Coco Masters, Carolina A. Miranda, and Tim Padgett, "The Men Who Dropped the Bombs," *Time*, August 1, 2005.

Greg Mitchell, "A Hole in History: America Suppresses the Truth About Hiroshima," *Progressive*, August 1995.

Lance Morrow, "Hiroshima and the Time Machine," *Time*, September 19, 1994.

Michael Novak, "Hiroshima 1983," *National Review*, October 28, 1983.

Gerald Parshall, "Shock Wave," *U.S. News & World Report,* July 31, 1995.

Norman Polmar and Thomas B. Allen, "The Bomb Minimized Casualties," *Technology Review*, August-September, 1995.

Thomas Powers, "Was It Right?" *Atlantic Monthly*, July 1995.

Alex Roland, "Keep the Bomb," *Technology Review,* August-September, 1995.

Roger Rosenblatt, "A Fire in the Sky; What the Boy Saw," *Time*, July 29, 1985.

Steve Rothman, "The Publication of 'Hiroshima' in *The New Yorker*," http://herseyhiroshima.com, January 8, 1997.

Murray Sayle, Virginia Hamilton Adair, and John Burnside, "Did the Bomb End the War?" *New Yorker,* July 31, 1995.

Martin L. Sherwin, "Hiroshima and Modern Memory," *Nation*, October 10, 1981.

Ronald Takaki, "What Scientists Knew and When They Knew It," *Technology Review*, August-September, 1995.

Evan Thomas and Osborn Elliott, "Why We Did It," *Newsweek*, July 24, 1995.

Time, "Report from Nagasaki," March 14, 1949.

Websites

Atomic Archive (www.atomicarchive.com). A comprehensive site covering the history surrounding the atomic bomb in detail, including a large collection of historic documents.

Atomic Heritage Foundation (www.atomicheritage.org). A nonprofit organization dedicated to the preservation and interpretation of the Manhattan Project and the Atomic Age and its legacy.

The Decision to Drop the Atomic Bomb (www.trumanlibrary. org/whistlestop/study_collections/bomb/large). A section of the Harry S. Truman Memorial Library and Museum containing scans of original documents related to the decision totaling almost 600 pages, plus photographs, oral histories, and the complete text of *Truman and the Bomb: A Documentary History*.

Hiroshima and Nagasaki Remembered (www.hiroshima-remembered.com). A project of the National Science Foundation's National Science Digital Library, including photos, videos, and scans of original documents as well as historical narratives, biographies, and links to other online resources.

Hiroshima Peace Memorial Museum (www.pcf.city.hiroshima. jp/top_e.html). The English version of the museum's website, containing information about its exhibits and Hiroshima's recovery, plus links and material advocating the abolition of nuclear weapons.

History @ Los Alamos (www.lanl.gov/history). A part of the Los Alamos National Laboratory site containing descriptions of the development of the atomic bomb at Los Alamos, life there during that era, and the Trinity test, including many photographs.

The Manhattan Project, An Interactive History (www.cfo.doe. gov/me70/manhattan). A site produced by the US Department of Energy's Office of History and Heritage Resources containing detailed history of events; sections on notable people and scientific achievements are being added gradually.

INDEX